THE LIFE OF BRIAN

The Life of Brian

The Brian Marwood Story

Brian Marwood
with
Brian Woolnough

MAINSTREAM
PUBLISHING

First published in Great Britain 1990 by
MAINSTREAM PUBLISHING COMPANY
(EDINBURGH) LTD
7 Albany Street
Edinburgh EH1 3UG

British Library Cataloguing in Publication Data
Marwood, Brian
    Life of Brian: the Brian Marwood story.
    1. England. Association football. Biographies
    I. Title   II. Woolnough
    796.334092

ISBN 1 85158 367 X

Typeset in 11/13 Imprint by Bookworm Typesetting Ltd, Edinburgh
Printed and bound in Great Britain by Billings & Sons, Worcester

Dedicated to my wife Lesley and children Charlotte, Sophie and James. For all their love and support, they help keep me sane.

CONTENTS

Introduction
THE WAY IT IS

HOWARD WILKINSON had almost finished his team meeting. It was ten to three in the Sheffield Wednesday dressing-room and we were lined up by the door to go out and face Coventry in a First Division match. There was nothing new about the scene: the air was full of the smells of lotion and the expectancy of success, the noise came from balls bouncing, players shouting encouragement to one another and the distant cheers and chants of the supporters.

Wilkinson, a man with a deep love for football and a wild passion to succeed, walked in and out of the players, punching his fist into the palm of his other hand, offering advice, raising his voice and generally pumping us up for the battle ahead. Then he stopped in front of John Pearson, our young striker. "It is a tough game for you today, lad," he said. "You're up against Brian Kilcline and he doesn't take any prisoners. This is the kind of treatment you can expect." With that Wilkinson drew back his hand and slapped Pearson's face!

Pearson stumbled and for a split second there was stunned silence. The noise and banter stopped and the players looked open-mouthed at the manager. None of us had seen anything like this before. But Wilkinson's timing was perfect and as Pearson regained his composure the whistle from the referee's dressing-room went and we had to file out on to the pitch.

Ninety minutes later we had beaten Coventry 1-0 and Pearson scored the only goal of the game. The incident was never mentioned again.

Yet that slap, that split second, had a massive effect on me. I hadn't seen or experienced anything like it. I was the kid from the sticks at Hull still with stars in his eyes. One or two of my managers at Hull had got angry, but to hit one of the team? Never. I thought about it a lot that night and wondered why Wilkinson had done it. Or, more importantly, why had he needed to slap Pearson. And it wasn't a playful slap, as it was delivered with the coldness of a man who knew exactly what he was doing.

The longer I played for Sheffield Wednesday and Howard Wilkinson, the more answers I discovered. I had never played for a manager like this man before. Nothing mattered to him except success. Not only for himself, but for the club, his staff and the supporters. He did things with and to the players that pushed us beyond the bounds of normal endurance, fitness, and motivation.

The demands on himself and the team are the reasons he hit Pearson. He believed that shock treatment would get the best out of the player on that occasion. There were other incidents, many amazing, that Howard used to push Sheffield Wednesday as far as possible.

From the day as a teenager when I chose to turn professional footballer rather than seek a career in cricket with Northamptonshire, I have sought out wise people to listen to. I like passion in people, I respect men who love football and want it to succeed as a profession. From an early age I realised that I didn't have the high level of natural skill that would take me right to the top automatically, so I decided that I would roll up my sleeves and work damn hard to get there. Along the way there have been many characters who

In action during our Championship season.

have influenced me, and Wilkinson is one of them. For a spell at Hillsborough the players were his disciples, we became clones of the manager. Yet, somehow, I respect him for what he was trying to achieve, and still is now at Leeds. Howard once said to us, "You will either like me or respect me", and he never changed course from that policy.

My burning ambition was always to get to the top and play for a big club and there have been other men who have helped me reach each step of the ladder of success. I will never forget Jimmy Dyson, a big man in more ways than one, who has remained a friend from my cricket days in the Durham Senior League, or Billy Bly, a giant of a "father-figure" who helped me when I was struggling to cope with life at Hull. But I probably owe more to Dennis Booth than anyone else. Dennis never made it to the top level in the game and yet he talked more sense than anyone in football I have met. We just hit it off from day one and I spent hours at his home in Hull after training just listening to and picking up things he said about the game. He became like a brother to me and I will always be grateful to him for his time and knowledge. I hope I repaid some of his kindness when I gave him the only England shirt I won. It was Dennis's dream to play for his country and I knew I had made a friend happy when he broke down with emotion as I presented him with the shirt I won in Saudi Arabia with England.

I so desperately wanted to add England manager Bobby Robson to the list of men whom I have grown to respect. Sadly, he let me down badly. He picked me up and then discarded me like an unwanted toy without a word of explanation. I will never know why he chose me in the first place and then gave me just nine minutes as a substitute. I didn't think it was a particularly impressive way to manage and I would like to think that if or when I become a manager I will be big enough to tell the truth to all players. All any professional footballer wants is honesty from his manager.

I'm sure I will be adding Gordon Taylor to my list of wise men. Here is a man who cares about football and its future. It hurts him to see the game suffer from his seat as chief executive of the Professional Footballers Association, the players' own union. I have started to work closely with the PFA and I know just how hard Gordon works for the development of football in this country. The players should realise how lucky they are to have him at the head of their organisation.

There have, of course, been others who have helped me in my search to gain success and taste the big time. It started out as a dream and then people like Dyson, Bly and Booth, helped me turn it into a reality.

Today Brian Marwood is a very proud man. My father once told me, "Never have regrets", and I can't say that I have many when I look back at my career at Hull, Hillsborough and Highbury. When you play for a club like Arsenal it would be easy to sit back and think, "That's it, I have made it." But I am only just starting. I am 30 years old with new mountains to climb and I don't feel any different to when I kicked my first ball in the professional game. My attitude remains: there is a lot of work to do and I am going to work flat out to get what I want.

Chapter One
THE WISE MEN

IT WAS Peter Willey, the England batsman and former Northants skipper who now plays for Leicester, who persuaded me to become a footballer rather than go into cricket. Willey warned me that unless you were a very successful cricketer it was an extremely lonely and lowly paid profession. For six months a year most players had to find alternative employment and at that time, in 1975, Willey was the groundsman at Northampton Town Football Club.

I appreciated his advice because it would have been easy for me to turn my back on soccer and sign for Northants. I had been having football trials with Hull and they were keen to sign me but I was swaying towards cricket and Northants. It was a dilemma for me and not an easy decision for a young boy to make. Willey did me a favour when he sat me down after a cricket dinner at my local club, Seaham Harbour, near to Sunderland in the north-east of England, and spelt out the "dos and don'ts" of cricket.

Willey had also played for Seaham Harbour and moved up the ranks, and he was the first person I knew who had really made it to the top – something I desperately wanted. I was brought up in Seaham, a real mining community, and I had made up my mind from an early age that I didn't want to follow my father Robert down the pits. It seemed to be the natural step for all the boys I played with and yet I knew that it wasn't for me. I was lucky enough to be blessed with enough basic sporting skill to break away from a career that I had no love of, or interest in.

It was cricket, ironically, which gave me my first insight into the harsh reality of professionalism. I played in the Durham Senior League and that is a competition which attracts good players from home and abroad. One man I came up against was Wasim Raja, the Pakistan test all-rounder. Wasim knew he was better than most of the players in the League and he decided to take it out on me to prove it. In one particular game he gave me "the treatment". In a Northants trial I had once faced a quick bowler called Jim Walker and thought that he was something special but Wasim could bowl all sorts, quick, medium, spin and then whizz one past your ears. He coupled this with a verbal assault. You know the stuff: "You can't play, I'll get you next time." It worked and by the end of the game I was a nervous wreck. Someone asked me if I got any runs and I had to say no, only down my leg!

The skipper of our side was big Jimmy Dyson, a mountain of a man who hated too much intimidation. He had seen all this going on throughout the day. So at the end of play Jimmy marched into the opposition's dressing-room, picked up Wasim and hung him on a coat peg by his shirt-collar. Some who experienced the incident said that was the first time they had seen a black man go white! Jimmy and I have remained friends ever since.

Strangely, I didn't really feel upset about Wasim's behaviour and I almost respected what he was trying to do. He was the professional and knew he was a better player than anyone else in the game and it was his way of showing his strength. Professionalism, I have since discovered, is part and parcel of top-level sport and verbal batterings are commonplace in cricket and football today. Not a minute goes by in the First Division without a player trying to intimidate an opponent

Peter Willey, the former test star and the man who persuaded me to play football and not cricket, hands me an award at a cricket function in Seaham.

with a cutting comment and, yes, I have often used the tactic myself.

Wasim's behaviour and Dyson's reaction taught me my first lesson: ever since that day I have tried to make the most of any situation. If things go wrong, I try to analyse why, or dissect a person's behaviour. I have always attempted to find good out of bad throughout my career in football.

Football was in my blood and from an early age I became steeped in Sunderland. I was brought up on players like Billy Hughes, Dennis Tueart, Mick Horswill and Ian Porterfield. I played with Horswill and almost signed for Porterfield later in my career and it was a great thrill to talk to both men because Sunderland meant a lot to me. The club was and will always be close to my heart. I have always said that I would walk on broken glass to play for Sunderland and that still applies. I dream of becoming their manager one day.

You had to be living in Sunderland in 1973 to realise the impact the club winning the FA Cup had on the area. It was a passion and excitement that grown men and women had never experienced before. Enemies became friends, strangers linked arms and industry picked up because people were happy to go to work. As they worked they discussed Sunderland Football Club, and time flew.

In the third round 'we' beat Notts County after a replay and had to go to a second game to get past Reading in the fourth round. The interest just boiled up. The fifth round brought in Manchester City and all their stars, Mike Summerbee, Colin Bell, Rodney Marsh and Francis Lee. Sunderland drew 2-2 at Maine Road and then beat them in yet another replay at Roker Park in front of 51,782 fans. It was one less by the end because I ended up in hospital after getting crushed against a crash barrier.

Sunderland by now was gripped in FA Cup fever. A home draw in the quarter final against Luton, and 53,151 saw Dave Watson and Ron Guthrie score the goals to take the club into a semi-final clash with Arsenal at Hillsborough. My parents wouldn't allow me to go to the game and I was pinned to the radio to listen to Sunderland's memorable 2-1 victory. "Away the lads!"

Seaham Harbour Cricket Club – those were the days.

It was the same for the final at Wembley against Leeds. I was one of the few who stayed behind to watch it on television and I can still see Ian Porterfield shooting Sunderland into the record books. Great days, great memories. It is difficult to describe the feeling of North-East people unless you were there, but it generated the same atmosphere as when England won the World Cup in 1966.

Sunderland's success put the area on the map as far as football was concerned. Scouts from top clubs started to pour into the area to watch youngsters, and exciting talent started to leave. Terry Fenwick signed for Malcolm Allison at Crystal Palace, Micky Hazard went to Spurs, I joined Hull and others were being noticed.

My breakthrough into the professional game came when a man called George Walker, a Hull scout who was also a prison officer at Durham Jail, approached me and asked me if I would be interested in going to Boothferry Park for trials. Hull's interest sparked a reaction of resentment from Seaham Boys, who selected kids from four or five schools in the area but had been overlooking me. Yet, as soon as I started to talk to Hull they wanted me, and one man, Bob Walton, even told me that he would stop me playing cricket and football altogether!

I signed for Hull when I was 14 years old, and the then manager, John Kaye, paid me the compliment of pulling me out of a trial game after just 20 minutes and telling me, "You have done enough, son. Get changed."

Once you have signed schoolboy forms you can't go anywhere else for two years, and then you are offered apprentice professional terms at 16 for another two years, if the club believe you are going to make the grade. The same rules apply today. Then, of course, comes the big decision every club must make: do they want to take the 18-year-old on full professional terms?

I was happy to sign for Hull and the reality was that I had nothing to compare it with. They were the only professional club to show interest in me and Hull, then in the Second Division, represented the first rung of the ladder for me. However, I would advise any boy today to compare and look at all the options if they are lucky enough to be offered trials and terms with more than one club. My alternatives were the Seaham pits and so I signed for Hull, determined to make a success of my footballing life.

At this stage I didn't realise or appreciate what an influence my father had been on my career. He had managed a local side when he was younger, and had seen a lot of potential footballers ruined by their fathers' selfish attitudes and demands. He had made a promise to himself never to fall into the same trap. There were times when I couldn't understand his background approach and I often wanted him to push me harder than he did. Yet he was always there, giving me advice and telling me when I had failed, or when to stand on my own two feet. I often played in representative matches hurt that my father wasn't watching, only to discover later that he had slipped into the ground and stood at the back. It was his way of dealing with the situation and now I respect what he did for me. He was a pillar of strength without me realising it at the time.

It had to be football for me because I was so preoccupied with my desire to succeed in sport, that I allowed my school studies to fall by the wayside. My school report at Seaham

Comprehensive continually read: "If Brian could show as much dedication to studies as he does to sport, he will go far." I regret it now, and I have made up for lack of qualifications at school since, but again I would advise any boy today to learn by my mistake and make sure he works hard off the playing field, and gains every qualification he can. This is something the PFA support and encourage.

When it was time to go out into the big wide world I was definitely ready for it. I had always been close to my family and yet I knew the time had come to stand on my own two feet and fend for myself. My mother, Eleanor, was broken-hearted and I can remember feeling sick with mixed emotions when my brother-in-law drove me from Seaham to Hull one Sunday afternoon to get settled into my first digs. It was what I wanted and not even a bad experience with my first landlady drove me back home.

Every footballer has their favourite landlady story and I am no exception. Mine had just split up from her husband and had taken in lodgers for the first time. But my fellow Hull apprentice, a lad called Eddie Hamilton, and I took weeks to realise what was going on when we returned home at the weekend. Even seeing her with black eyes and a cut lip on Monday morning had not convinced us that there were problems. Only when things started to disappear from our rooms did we discover that her husband was returning while we were not there, ransacking the house and beating her up. It was the excuse we needed to get out because the food had been terrible, and we even had to put 50p in the television to keep it going!

I firmly believe that between the ages of 16 and 18 you need a settled environment and I was lucky enough at that age to meet a fellow called Billy Bly, a former professional goalkeeper who played cricket with me for a team called the Hull Tigers. Bly turned out to be my 'guardian angel' and he literally took me under his wing in those early days away from home. I needed a stable base and Bly became a substitute father to me. I stayed with him and his wife; he was a shoulder to cry on, an experienced head to bounce ideas off, and I will always be grateful to him. It broke my heart when he died.

He never once saw me play football, despite helping mould my career.

It's tough at the bottom and in those early days at Hull my job was to clean boots, paint the ground, sweep terraces and tidy the first-team dressing-room. Billy Bremner, the former captain of Leeds and Scotland, had arrived at Hull and it was also my responsibility to clean his boots, all ten pairs of them! Bremner gave me a terrible rollicking one day because I had only cleaned his match boots and not the nine other pairs. I thought to myself: "What an arrogant bastard. You'll get your comeuppance." Sure enough, he did, and he fell out with his good friend, another Leeds old boy, Bobby Collins over it.

When John Kaye was sacked as Hull manager the job was between Bremner and Collins and they obviously discussed the situation as they travelled together from Leeds every day. Bremner was interviewed first and I understand he was dismayed when he discovered that the board were insisting on having a say over team matters. Bremner's reaction was, quite rightly, no way. Collins, however, came out of the room after five minutes with the job, and there is no question that they lost respect for one another after that. I don't know whether they are still friends today.

Bobby Collins was a good coach and handled players superbly but when he got the manager's job he just couldn't cope with the new role. He seemed to suffer a massive inferiority complex, which was surprising for a player who had strutted around with the arrogant air of someone who didn't have a care in the world. I can remember the coach driver coming into the club one morning and saying: "I don't believe it, the manager has just asked me what I think the team should be?"

Collins went from being someone who was close to the players to being a distant stranger. It is a transition that a lot of people have trouble in coping with. You don't make a good manager just because you have been a successful player, while great managers are often those who never made it to the top as a player. Dennis Booth, my best mate and someone I will always respect, is the perfect example. Dennis is a coach, a real players' man. I think personally he would find it hard to pull himself away from the players, and be a manager. I firmly

Happy days at Hull and a trip to Scarborough. My best mate Dennis Booth is on the right, second row back.

believe that you must stand back from your staff, even become cold in their eyes. George Graham at Arsenal is a great example of this. He was, I'm told, a good mixer when he was playing, and enjoyed a night out with the lads, but as a manager no one knows George Graham.

I had seven managers at Hull: John Kaye, Bobby Collins, Ken Houghton (another former player who found it hard to adapt), Mike Smith (the former Wales manager who gave me my debut, against Mansfield on 12 January 1980), Chris Chiltern, Colin Appleton and Brian Horton.

Smith made a big impression on me. He had been a national manager and brought his first-class attitude and ideas to the club. I was ready to launch my career in the first team and I liked this man who wanted to turn the club upside down. He brought with him Cyril Lea, the former Ipswich coach and his right-hand man with Wales, and he wanted the best for the players. We found ourselves on executive coaches, in the best hotels and on better contracts. The complaint had always been that Hull lacked ambition and yet Smith desperately tried to go the other way.

We fought hard against relegation but that didn't dampen his enthusiasm or his spending, and it was soon clear that he was costing the club a lot of money. He once enthused to us about the new washing machines he had installed at the club and the reaction from some Hull people was obvious: "Who cares about clean shirts? What about the results?"

Dennis Booth was once called into Smith's office and he was surprised to see a secretary sitting alongside Smith's big, impressive desk, a cleaner tidying up and a decorator painting the ceiling. "Dennis," Smith said, "things are leaking out of this club and I want to know who is responsible." Dennis just looked around and thought to himself that Smith was either naïve or blind. That was Mike, however, and he was probably too nice for his own good. He wanted the best of everything and failed to accept the harsh reality of running a Third Division football club.

A manager's nightmare began to take shape as players' cliques started to form inside the club. The more I became involved with the first team, the more I realised what a bad environment it was. When you are not doing well it is harder, because people take advantage. In football there are always a lot of enemies waiting to kick you when you are down. In that 1979-80 season we avoided relegation to Division Four by just one point, and it was interesting to note who finished bottom of the Third that year – Wimbledon, with just ten wins and 34 points all season. What a fantastic comeback in the Eighties therefore, by the club that everyone loves to hate.

It was during that season that Dennis Booth began to have a great impact on me. At the age of 20 I took strength from his character, especially after the Hull fans tried to destroy him and then warmed to his personality. I used his knowledge of the game to help improve my own standing as a person and player.

Dennis never made it to the top as a player and yet he retained this wonderful passion for the game. He once told me: "When I have to retire it will be like cutting off my arms and legs." At the time I thought what a stupid thing to say because even after playing you have your whole life ahead of you but the more I got to know him the more I knew what he meant. Football is his lifeblood and without it he wouldn't be the same person. He once told me that the highlight of his career was when his former Watford team-mate Luther Blissett gave him a pair of England socks. It was always Booth's dream to represent his country and that is why I gave him my shirt after my one and only England appearance. He has put it in pride of place in his home, nicely mounted and I am delighted to use that as a thank you for all he has done for me.

The following season, 1980-81, we were relegated to Division Four; and it was a miserable time for me. We finished rock bottom behind Blackpool, Colchester and Sheffield United. I scored four goals from 40 games in my first full season as a league player but it meant nothing to me. There was a deep depression hanging over the club and the players knew something had to happen.

Hull is an area of England that is a hotbed for Rugby League. The football club is definitely the poor relation, and that is exactly how we felt at that time. By February 1982 it was announced that the club was to go into liquidation, and that had a devastating effect on everyone, particularly the players. Mike Smith had parted company, and there was a tremendous amount of confusion and depression inside the club. I met Gordon Taylor then for the first time. On one of his visits he tried to put into perspective what was happening. It wasn't easy for him, as people like the chairman, Christopher Needler, saw a family tradition disappearing in front of his eyes.

There were numerous team meetings, led by skipper Mick Horswill, my old hero from Sunderland. At one stage the players simply had enough, and we disappeared into the local pub to drown our sorrows. We were playing matches, and yet, for what reason? It seemed as if it was just a matter of time before Hull City FC rolled over and died. That gathering in the pub seemed to be the beginning of the end. We were saying goodbye to a section of our careers, and none of us knew what the future held.

The club had told us, through the PFA and Gordon Taylor, that we would all get free transfers at the end of the season and I began to get one or two telephone calls from interested managers. Colin Murphy at Lincoln, and Luton's David Pleat both spoke to me on the telephone. Pleat was the more persuasive and I arranged to speak to him at a hotel one Friday. I asked Dennis Booth if he would come along as my advisor as I had no experience of transfer talk or contracts and discussing a move with a manager was to be a new experience for me. Pleat, however, had guessed that I would bring a friend, and he had arranged for Brian Horton, Luton's skipper and an old friend of Booth, to meet him in the reception area as we walked in. So while Brian and Dennis chattered downstairs I was whisked upstairs to talk over a possible move to Luton.

I wasn't particularly against the idea of moving to Luton. They were a progressive Second Division club and David Pleat's reputation as one of the bright managers of the future was growing with every season. And I was stuck in the Fourth Division with a club heading for the scrapheap.

Gordon Taylor had given me some advice before I travelled to meet Pleat and although I was allowed to talk to anyone, he advised me not to sign a contract at that particular stage. Pleat had a contract in the room and explained that he had Football

League permission to sign me. "There is no problem," he said. "Sign this and no one can do a thing about it." It was tempting but I refused and said that I would go home to discuss the move and that I would let him know.

I don't know whether it was fate or just lucky judgment but within a few days there was more hope at Hull. The club woke up to the fact that good players were on the brink of being sold for nothing and they made a boardroom decision to demand transfer fees for players. Luton had not been prepared to pay a fee for me and so I was stuck with seeing my contract out at Hull.

All the players were still together and the crisis of the occasion definitely rallied us. We found a terrific spirit within the camp and started to even pull away from the bottom of the Fourth Division with a run of results that was promotion form. The results and points were gained, of course, to a background of mounting problems off the field. We may have been winning but the future of the club was still in doubt. Everyone knew that Hull City needed a miracle. Something had to happen.

It did. Doctor Death came into our lives.

Chapter Two

FROM HULL TO HILLSBOROUGH

I HAVE made some great friends and met some amazing characters in my career – Jimmy Dyson, Billy Bly, Dennis Booth, Howard Wilkinson – but Doctor Death came and went like a tornado tearing through my life.

Don Robinson is the kind of guy you probably only meet once in your lifetime. He is one of those characters whose motto is: I can achieve anything. And he went about his business with a sledgehammer, knocking everything and everyone out of his way until he got what he wanted. He was nicknamed Doctor Death from his prowess as a former wrestler but there were many more strings to his bow. The biggest was confidence and it helped him in his career as an entrepreneur. He began his money-making empire in Scarborough and was linked to a theme park, an opera house and many more show-stopping events. It seemed whatever he touched turned to gold, even if you were never quite sure exactly how he made it all work.

Football was his latest craze and after failing to buy his way into Hartlepool and Halifax Robinson arrived at Hull like a knight in shining armour. He turned the club on its head and, yes, we were happy to see him.

Hull City needed a lift, and he provided it, as well as money, and everyone responded to the new owner and chairman. There was a smile back on the faces of the staff and supporters and the players reacted with a run that took us from close to the bottom of the Fourth Division to about eighth. Everyone had been negative in their approach to the future until he arrived but Robinson literally took us by the scruff of the neck and hauled the club up the table with his enthusiasm. The man had been used to getting his own way after building up his empire from nothing and nobody at Hull felt like standing in his way. In fact, Doctor Death was encouraged to cast his spell.

He stabilised the club financially and swept it into a new era. It is amazing how many mixed emotions I had experienced in such a short time as a professional footballer. Relegation, liquidation, almost losing my job, almost signing for Luton and now the excitement of a bright future. Robinson claimed that Hull could reach the top and for a time we all believed him. It was hard not to get emotionally attached to the only professional club I had known.

Chris Chiltern, a former Hull player, had taken over from Mike Smith but Robinson wanted his own man and Colin Appleton, who had already worked for the new chairman at Scarborough, arrived. Like most things Robinson touched, it turned to gold and we were promoted that season, 1982-83. We finished second, eight points behind champions Wimbledon, and I was top scorer from my midfield position with 19 goals, including three penalties.

Life was great at that time. In the summer of 1983 I married my fiancée, Lesley, a lovely girl I had met two years earlier from our home town of Seaham. Lesley was qualifying as a chiropodist. I was still in digs in Hull but we met up as frequently as we could, although it was mainly at the weekends when team-mate Billy Askew gave me a lift home in his battered old Capri. We journeyed back at six o'clock every Saturday night and met up again in the early hours of Monday morning to be in time for ten o'clock training at Hull. They were enjoyable days and I look back on them now with tremendous pleasure and pride.

The chairman even helped me buy a house after we were married when he lent me £3,000 of his own money to put down on a property in Beverley, a village close to Hull. I loved the man. I thought he was too good to be true – and eventually that did turn out to be the case.

The new season, 1983-84, brought more success and fun for the people of Hull. Under Appleton and Robinson we began as we had left off, winning matches and playing exciting football. John Bond's Burnley were the Third Division favourites and we beat them 4-1 on the opening day of the season. Lee Dixon, my Arsenal team-mate today and a good friend, played against me that day.

On 10 September 1983 we also smashed Millwall 5-0 at home. Their manager that day was none other than George Graham and I wonder if it was my performance, especially my goal, that jogged his memory when he eventually signed me from Sheffield Wednesday.

Hull hit top spot after that victory over Graham's Millwall and though it was the only day we went ahead of the rest it looked as though we were going to run straight through the division. We hardly moved out of the top five all season and chairman Robinson celebrated at Christmas by going on to the pitch before the kick-off, dressed in a white cowboy hat, on a white stallion, and charging around the track, handing out cigars to the fans.

The supporters loved it and so did we. He brought a feeling of class to the club and made sure that everything was paid for when we travelled and stayed overnight. He liked style and wanted everyone associated with him to live life to the full. We even made a record, something that is normally reserved for cup final teams or national World Cup sides. Robinson didn't care – if it got him publicity, he tried it.

It started to go wrong when we were due to play away at Burnley in midwinter and our coach driver found it impossible to get over the Pennines and down into Burnley.

The match had to be called off, despite the conditions being fine in Burnley, and the club was fined for failing to fulfil a fixture. It was rearranged for the last game of the season.

The Burnley incident seemed to knock us out of our stride and after hitting a sticky patch at Easter we ended up by having to go to Turf Moor for that last match needing to win 3-0 to get promotion. After playing so well and achieving so much, it was a knife-edge situation. It was a midweek game and the ground was packed with supporters all nursing mixed emotions. Our fans were desperate for glory. Burnley, of course, wanted to stop us and there was a big gathering from Sheffield United, our rivals who went up if we failed.

We murdered Burnley, I scored twice and yet we couldn't get a third. We hit the bar, the post, had shots cleared off the line and did everything but take Hull City into the Second Division. It was one of those nights and one I will never forget – for the wrong reasons. Football grips you with emotion on many occasions and this was another experience for me. It was frustration and bitter disappointment.

On the way home I thought about the penalty I had missed at Oxford, the team who ended up as Champions,

One of the worst nights of my life. I score twice at Burnley for Hull, this is the first, but we miss out on promotion by one goal.

and thought . . . if only. I didn't sleep that night because promotion was such a huge thing to miss out on. I felt part of Hull and, after all that had gone on under Robinson, I just refused to believe that we had experienced failure.

It is amazing how quickly it all changed. Within minutes of us failing to gain promotion Colin Appleton resigned. No one could believe it at the time but the stories started to emerge about how he had been let down by the chairman. Suddenly Don Robinson lost some of the polish from his shining armour. People began to question his motives and his approach to Hull. There had obviously been a lot going on between Colin and the chairman, and Appleton, a man of principle, quit. You had to admire him for going through with something he felt strongly about. It was claimed that Colin had been paid peanuts for working around the clock for Hull and he decided that he just couldn't stomach the situation any longer. Had we won promotion he may have reconsidered and even discussed new terms with Robinson but the disappointment of failing at the last hurdle was too much to cope with.

It made me consider my own future. I was happy at Hull and yet was this the club to take me on to the kind of prizes I wanted to win? It would be a wrench to leave after experiencing so much but I had to think of my career. There were whispers about Sheffield United and Sheffield Wednesday being interested and I decided that if the club came to me and said that they had accepted a firm offer I would go.

There were also doubts about Hull climbing the mountain again after going so close. Had we won promotion there is no way I would have considered quitting the club. I desperately wanted them to succeed because they were part of me, and always will be. However, I now made it known that I wanted to go and my mind was made up for me when the club only offered me the same terms for the following season. I thought that was a disgrace, considering I had been top scorer for two successive seasons and had cost Hull nothing. Appleton's problems with the chairman suddenly began to fall into perspective.

Brian Horton had taken over as manager and one of his first jobs was to persuade me to stay. Brian, however, was another person I will always be grateful to because he drew on all his experience and admitted that the best thing for me was to play in the First Division. He told me: "I would love you to stay but I have experienced life in the First and Second and if you get a chance you must grab it." Dennis Booth was now coaching the first team and he gave me the same push in the right direction.

It was the obvious decision for me. I was now recognised as a good Third and Fourth Division player and desperately wanted to prove to myself that I could be a success at the very top. Wednesday, Sheffield United, Spurs, Watford and George Graham's Millwall were all said to be interested. I realised it was now or never for Brian Marwood. My next club had to be right. I take football extremely seriously. I am not in it for the booze or the night clubs. I am a professional and I want to succeed at the highest level. At that stage of my career it concerned me that I might be getting left behind. I was still looking up at the best clubs and players.

There was no way I was going to pack up and go back to Seaham and down the pits. The beauty of spells like those is that they help sort out a person's character and I like to believe that I am a fighter. When I was a junior player I spent hours on my own in the gym bashing a ball against the wall and controlling it with my feet and head when all the other players had gone home. I knew that I didn't have the natural skill, so I had to battle to achieve what I set out in my life's plan. My father had always told me: "Give life your best shot and hold your head up high. Never have regrets." He was right, of course, and it would have been easy for me at 18 to have turned around and gone back to a normal life in Seaham. It wasn't what I wanted however. I fought on and, with a new club on the horizon, I was determined to make sure I didn't make a mistake in choice.

It turned out to be Wednesday. I signed for them in June 1984 but not before I fell out in a big way with Doctor Death.

The fee for my transfer was to be settled by an Independent

Tribunal because Hull and Sheffield Wednesday couldn't agree on a fee. Wednesday had offered £80,000 while Robinson demanded £200,000. Whatever the fee, I was going to get an ex-gratia payment as a reward for my services to the club. So, when the fee was settled, Hull would write me out a cheque. Wednesday agreed, Robinson said yes, and I was happy because everyone accepted that after eight years' service and low wages it was a reward I deserved.

It was all above board and was to be written into my contract. The tribunal finally settled my fee at £115,000 and while it was more than Wednesday wanted to pay they signed the cheque and I looked forward to my new career in the First Division. The one problem was Robinson, who refused to cough up. He was disgusted with the low fee, said he was not paying me and even denied any agreement with me.

His decision and attitude left me with nothing to show for a long career with Hull. I still claim he had gone back on his word and left me high and dry. My only trump card was that I still had the £3,000 he loaned me for my house and before I left I hissed in his ear: "You have done this to me after giving so much for your football club, you can stick your £3,000. You are not getting that back." He demanded I return his money and we left having had a blazing row.

Later that season we met at the PFA dinner and he brought up his missing cash straight away. "You know you still owe me £3,000," he said and my reply was just as firm: "You cost me, stuff your money." The row seemed to upset Robinson and a few hours later he returned to my company, drink in hand, and said that he would write me out a cheque there and then for £10,000. I said no thanks and that the damage had been done.

At that time in my life I could have done with £10,000 but there was a principle at stake and I had learned enough from people I respect that principle and pride are not something you can put a price on. People have since told me that I should have taken the money yet not once have I regretted the decision.

The next time I saw Doctor Death was at an awards dinner at Hull the following season. He was in the middle of a big row with Colin Appleton. Times don't change but, like my dad told me, I can hold my head up high.

For the record, Hull were promoted to the Second Division the following season under Brian Horton and that is where they are today. Don Robinson is still the chairman and good luck to him. I hope he achieves what he wants in the rest of his life and I will certainly never forget him. But in my opinion the man let me down, badly.

It wasn't an easy decision to sign for Wednesday because their Sheffield neighbours and arch rivals, United, pushed me hard. Wednesday were the first to approach me but I had to listen to what United had to say, if only to have a discussion with their manager Ian Porterfield, one of my heroes from Sunderland and the man whose goal took the FA Cup to Roker.

Heroes are always held in esteem and then the image crumbles when you actually meet them. Ian, however, lived up to the picture I had painted and I was extremely impressed with everything United said and offered me. I spoke with the chairman Reg Brierley and they even offered to set Lesley up in her own business in the centre of Sheffield. It was tempting, especially as the money was better than the deal I had been offered at Hillsborough.

But the difference was First Division football and United were still in the Second. Had Ian Porterfield offered me First Division football I would have signed for United – there is no question about that. They were desperate for the big time and players like Peter Withe and Ken McNaught had been signed to prove the point. However, I had left Hull for one main reason and that was to play First Division football. That was what swayed me in the end. I went backwards and forwards to both clubs before giving a final yes to Howard Wilkinson. My heart wanted United, my head told me to go to Wednesday.

It is impossible not to be impressed with Howard Wilkinson when you first meet him. He demonstrates his passion and deep feeling for the game. In my first interview out came the blackboard and chalk, with Howard going through how Wednesday played and where he wanted me to fit into the side. I realised then just how much he loved Sheffield Wednesday and how he wanted them and him to be a success. I felt myself warming to him because I have always liked my football people to be full of passion and steeped in the game.

At last, I had arrived in the First Division and yes, I liked Wilkinson and wanted to play for him. I was ready for his methods of management . . . well, almost.

Chapter Three
HOWARD'S WAY

ON THE day that I signed for Sheffield Wednesday I had three hours to kill while I waited for my medical examinations to be completed. I sat in the dressing-room talking to the physiotherapist, Alan Smith, and even agreed to go on a run with him while we waited for the tests. Then in walked a man I grew to dislike.

They called Peter Eustace the squire of Stockbridge in Sheffield, a man who strutted around with an air of someone who thought he was important. Eustace, Howard Wilkinson's right-hand man, took one look at me and barked: "Hello, son, I'm Peter Eustace. I hope you are going to be fit because you are coming to a football club that demands fitness. If you are not, you won't last five minutes."

His arrogance and sheer presence hit me and I suppose you could say we clashed from day one.

Then when I went on my run with Smith I realised just how much fitness meant to Wilkinson's way of playing. If this was a friendly jog to waste a bit of time and to see where

A goal for Sheffield Wednesday and it puts Ipswich in the Second Division.

the Wednesday players did their training, what would the real thing be like? It didn't take me long to discover just how hard footballers train when the manager and his assistant have it in their minds to work players to their maximum limits. It was shock treatment and certainly brought me down to earth after I had spent a few days congratulating myself on becoming a First Division player, plus gaining all the trimmings that went with it.

A big plus for me was that Howard wanted me to play in my favourite position, alongside the front-line players with a free hand to go into dangerous areas. That had been a stumbling block at Sheffield United where Ian Porterfield had said that I would be an out-and-out winger, a position I had played in but not one I particularly enjoyed. Wednesday were also trebling my wages from Hull and Lesley and I moved into a new £50,000 house. I felt that I had arrived on the next rung of the ladder.

It would have been easy to have taken Sheffield United's bigger salary, and for the second time in my career, following Don Robinson's offer of £10,000, I turned down a payday. I knew, however, that ambition came first, and I expected to pick up bigger cash rewards if Wednesday were a success. I had arrived in the First Division and no matter what anyone said about what I had achieved in my career, I could say: "At least I played in the First Division."

It was certainly a big step up. I was the kid out of the backwater in Hull and suddenly I appeared under the media spotlight of a passionate football city. It felt like Sunderland back in the Seventies when I was a spectator, rather than a player involved. I was 24 years old and very naïve but I desperately wanted to look, learn and listen as I experienced life in the top drawer.

And did I learn the hard way. My biggest problem was fitness and I struggled like hell at the start to cope with the work Wednesday put in. Howard had just brought the club into the First Division and it seemed that most of his players had similar backgrounds. We were either new faces desperate to make a name for ourselves, or players who had been around a bit without ever pushing through the barrier of real success. Men like Lee Chapman, a striker who had threatened so much at Stoke, Arsenal and Sunderland without fulfilling his potential, Andy Blair, Lawrie Madden, Martin Hodge, Mel Sterland, Peter Shirtliff, Nigel Worthington, Gary Shelton and me had all been purposely hand-picked. We were grateful for the chance and Wilkinson moulded our football lives and, yes, our lives in general.

He ate, drank and slept football for Sheffield Wednesday and expected his staff to do the same. We had deep, meaningful meetings about football, behaviour, life . . . anything, and they went on for hours. We had meetings about meetings and not a day went by without the team getting together with the manager.

Then there was the training. Oh, that training! Never, never have I experienced anything like it. Amazingly, it didn't stop with just pre-season – we trained even harder throughout the winter.

In my first pre-season Lesley and I stayed at a hotel while our house was sorted out and I was so ill after a couple of days with the Wilkinson way I couldn't eat. Everything I tried to eat I just brought up. The stress and strain on my body was too much. It was all day and every day and I used to creep up to my bed at six o'clock praying that tomorrow wouldn't be so hard.

An average day began in the Derbyshire hills with non-stop running. Howard found routes even the rabbits hadn't discovered and they went on forever. Then it was back to the training ground for every method of physical build up. It was physical rather than skilful and that is the way Wilkinson wanted his assault on the First Division.

Howard liked to play non-league sides in our build up to the big kick-off but I didn't realise that the matches were scheduled for the evening after a full day in the hills and at the training ground. By the time we played the match my legs were like jelly and I simply couldn't run. I had a nightmare in those games. I couldn't stand up and began to question my own ability. On more than one occasion I thought I had made the wrong decision and that professional football perhaps wasn't the career for me.

Anything the players did, Wilkinson did too. He ran every route, joined in every game, did every exercise and expected his staff to be just as fit. Peter Eustace, Mick Hinnigan and Alan Smith were all there every day pounding the hills and the roads. You have seen those American army films when the sergeant runs alongside chanting instructions – that was us!

In the final friendly before that first season, 1984-85, I thought that at last we were finding our feet. In the game at Notts County things were improving. We were winning 1-0 and at half-time I expected Howard to be pleased. Instead he came into the dressing-room, picked up a cup of hot tea on the table and threw it across the room, smashing it into small pieces. It was the first time I saw Howard Wilkinson go berserk. It happened

many times after that and it was just part of his shock
treatment.

I had my eyes opened wide and the Wilkinson experience
never stopped me. He turned his moods on like a tap, one
minute he was rollocking us, the next he was the brilliant
deep-thinking football brain who couldn't be disturbed.

On one occasion Andy Blair, Lesley and I decided to
share a bottle of champagne with the gaffer to celebrate
the arrival of Andy's first baby. Howard's wife invited us
around to their house and we duly arrived full of excitement
and happiness for the Blairs. Howard, alas, had a few drinks
then moved to the corner of the room listening instead
to something on his headphones. It was extraordinary
behaviour by a very complex man. We never discovered
what he was listening to – music, football commentary, a
political speaker – who knows?

But that was Howard. He cared so much about football
and gaining success. He was also fussy about the way
his players behaved off the field and standards were
important.

In my opening season I struggled in the first matches
and was pulled off on more than one occasion. It was
simply down to finding my feet in the First Division and
coping with the extra demands of fitness. The team also
took time to find its feet. We began with a 3-1 home win
over Nottingham Forest, lost at Newcastle and Stoke and
then beat Southampton and Spurs at Hillsborough, with
me scoring my first Wednesday goal in the 2-1 victory over
Tottenham.

Howard would stop at nothing to make us better players
and improve the results for the club. He employed a
guy to video all our matches and compile a graph of
individual performances. Every detail was accounted for,
how many times you touched the ball, passes made,
tackles won. On a Monday morning the manager was
always full of details from Saturday's match and greeted
you with, "Brian, you only got two far post crosses in
on Saturday, that's not good enough." You couldn't argue
with him because it was all on video and down on his

graph. He must have spent hours on Sunday working it out.

He loved to analyse the human body and work out how higher peaks of fitness could be reached, or examine the right minerals each player's body required. He once prescribed a course of energy tablets for us that turned the urine a different colour. It began to worry a lot of us and the tablets all ended up in the River Don!

Despite his methods players still respected Howard Wilkinson. He was a football man with a deep feeling for the future of the sport and a passion for Sheffield Wednesday to succeed in the First Division. He was prepared to go to any extreme to reach his goal. The slapping of John Pearson was a classic example, the throwing of the cup, it was all part of the Wilkinson shock treatment. I was left in no doubt how he wanted me to perform. Before I kicked a ball for the club he gave me a video of a Sheffield Wednesday game with the instructions to watch it closely: "This is how we play," he said. "This is how I want you to play." For hours I watched Gary Bannister, the player I was to replace, and Imre Varadi, the player he wanted me to play with, and marvelled at their work rate. Before long I was just as committed, just as involved with the Wilkinson style.

In training, if anyone hit a ball less than 20 yards, it was a free kick. We were encouraged to hit the ball as long as possible and if a pass was neatly touched to feet the game was stopped and another free kick given! It went against the grain but it was Howard's Way. The back players knew that if they won the ball they had to deliver it without ceremony to the last third of the pitch, and usually into the areas by the corner flags.

The midfield players knew that it was no use "showing" in front of the back four, you just weren't going to collect the ball. Their job was to support the front men as Lee Chapman, Imre Varadi and I chased and fought for the long passes delivered over the opposing back four. It was a ruthless and uncomplicated tactic, but an effective one. There was a lot of pressure on Lee, the big man who had to battle and graft the entire game, often chasing lost causes.

My job was to give Wednesday width up front and pursue free areas. It was a role I enjoyed and who was Brian Marwood to complain? I had just fulfilled an ambition by playing in the First Division and while I had experienced nothing like this commitment, this style, this fitness, I was happy to be converted in a successful side. It was a big club doing well and I didn't want to rock the boat.

Then there was the controlled, physical side of Wednesday. Howard is a strict disciplinarian and he demands good on-field behaviour but there is no question that he likes his side to dominate the opposition. We had a defence who could definitely look after themselves and they were encouraged to "dig" for the good of the team. Men like Mel Sterland, Lawrie Madden, Peter Shirtliff, Mark Smith and Nigel Worthington can all look after themselves.

Howard felt that we could psyche out sides, especially at Hillsborough. Before the kick-off in the dressing-room we held hands and formed a circle while Howard encouraged us to think positive thoughts. There was silence while we tried to psyche ourselves up mentally. Who knows if the players took it seriously but we were encouraged all the time. Then came the "Diddley Dee" circle in the warm-up session as we shouted, roared and pushed ourselves to the peak of aggression for the game. You have seen the All Blacks do it before every International with their war chants – well that was Wednesday and Wilkinson.

The warm-ups in the dressing-room were often just as physical as the match itself. Mick Lyons used to stand in the middle of the room with a player in front of him and head the ball away as it was thrown to him from across the other side of the table. This was done non-stop for five minutes and more than once Lyons needed stitches in a cut forehead before he went out for the real battle.

On 29 September in that first season we went to Liverpool and won 2-0. It was a fantastic performance, although the thing I remember most was at half-time when Howard turned on me as I was being stitched up following an elbow in the face

43

from Liverpool's former England International full-back Phil Neal. Howard was furious that I had been hurt and before I went back out he said this is what you must do if he tries it on again and elbowed me full in the face, almost opening up my stitches! I was temporarily stunned but it was just more shock treatment from an extraordinary manager. It was harsh professionalism from the manager and, again, I had not experienced anything like it before.

Wilkinson, however, didn't elbow me or slap Pearson to hurt us in the true sense of the word. It was part of his way of bringing the best out in a team. He didn't want Liverpool to get one over on one of his players and he refused to believe that Wednesday were second best. It was his way of telling us how to look after ourselves.

We did become tougher mentally, more aware of the physical needs of the First Division. And, yes, sides were intimidated. Before every game we finished our war cry by

I score against Liverpool in Wednesday's first season back in the First Division.

44

running down the tunnel screaming and shouting on to the pitch. On 30 October, Leicester came to Hillsborough and didn't want to know. They were thrashed 5-0.

For a long period we became Wilkinson clones, the disciples of a man who was preaching a game I knew nothing about.

Howard, as you can imagine, was fiercely loyal to his players. The media were always on his back and he received tremendous criticism about the way Sheffield Wednesday played the game. There is no doubt that he stayed with the long-ball system against the wishes of many people. At Christmas, however, he arranged a lunch for the local and national newspaper men and purposely forgot to tell them that all the players would be there. You can just picture the scene. After a few glasses of Christmas wine the players got stuck into the press and gave them a taste of their own medicine. It was a clever move by the manager and a glimpse of his quick-witted, sharp brain and his loyalty.

One supporter couldn't believe what was happening to him one Monday morning when Howard arrived on his doorstep with Lee Chapman. Howard pressed the door bell and said to the guy, "You don't think he can play, tell him to his face." The fan had written a letter in the local sports paper, criticising Lee, and before training Howard grabbed Chapman and took him across Sheffield in his car to confront the critic. Chappie was embarrassed and the poor bloke was gobsmacked.

That was Wilkinson: unpredictable, fiercely competitive but extremely loyal. He was also a very honest man and despite his dour appearance, an eloquent, nice person.

There were many changes of mood and he couldn't stand players who tried to cheat on him. Once Carl Shutt was struggling in training and Howard caught him walking at the back of the pack. Carl immediately had his session doubled.

The physical and mental strain on the players was enormous. It seems amazing now when I look back

back and yet I lived through it and, in a funny way, enjoyed the experience.

Howard didn't like many Southern clubs. He didn't respect their way of life and he once called Tottenham a load of "fat cats and fancy dans" after one visit to London. He didn't believe they were committed enough to the cause and often conceded that he was disgusted with their attitude. He didn't like the way London clubs threw money around either. I would like to talk to him now that he is at Leeds for, in my opinion, his new club have bought their way to Second Division promotion. I wonder if somewhere along the line something or someone made his attitude change?

I was substituted four times in the first six matches as I struggled to cope with the demands of a new way of life. Peter Eustace didn't help. He was continually on my back about not being fit enough and I had to dig deep into my character to get through those early months. It was a good test for me and I was determined to beat it. I had signed a three-year contract and at the end of that period had my heart set on being an established First Division player.

Our results were rather like the manager's mood – they changed quickly and without warning. After beating Leicester we were second, then we lost at Coventry and at home to Norwich, only to bounce back with a victory over Arsenal. And the training never let off!

A typical week in the season under Howard began with the players piling into a minibus for the journey across Sheffield to the reservoir. Win, lose or draw on Saturday we knew what to expect on Monday.

Howard's attitude was that if a match lasted 90 minutes that is how long you should run for and we did, pounding the pavements until every bone and joint in our legs ached. By the time I got in the bath I could hardly walk, my ankles and knees were that sore.

Some of the players would try to feign an injury to escape from the hell of Monday morning and yet the physio was just as committed. With Alan Smith you worked from nine to five doing weights, bike, having treatment and body exercises. There was no escape – it was hard physical work wherever you turned.

Tuesday and more running. This time up into the Derbyshire hills and often non-stop. There were cross-country routes, runs through the woods, runs up hills and down dales, runs you didn't know existed.

Wednesday, at last, and a day off. You spent your rest day doing just that, resting. No golf or shopping with your wife. Howard was happy if you kept your feet up and simply got enough energy for the rest of the week's build-up.

With forty-eight hours to go before the next match Howard would at last start building up in a different way. He would begin to concentrate on the opposition and their strengths and weaknesses. He would explain how we were going to cope with individuals and he would pick out the danger areas of their side. He was usually spot on. There was plenty of ball work on a Thursday and it always concentrated around beating our next opponents, shadow play, dead ball and free kicks.

The start of the week was physical, the second half of the week often turned into a mental strain. Before training he spoke about the opposition for an hour and while other clubs have a light Friday and finish about midday we were working towards the next day's match at one-thirty and two o'clock in the afternoon.

The players had confidence in Wilkinson because his reading of a match was superb and he knew how to combat most effectively the strengths of the best sides in the division. Against Liverpool, for instance, we played with three front men and the two wide players were ordered to cut off their full-backs. That left Chappie on his own to battle against Alan Hansen and Gary Gillespie, with the surprise coming when midfield players were sprung from their area of the game into the path of the Liverpool central defenders. He didn't want Hansen and Gillespie to have room or time to play and our results against Liverpool at that time proved what a shrewd reader of the game Wilkinson is. Similarly, when we played Nottingham Forest there was always a plan set for Nigel Clough in his deep striker's role. Wilkinson's attitude was to nullify their danger and earn the right for us to introduce our power play.

Howard had worked out via his videos and graphs that we scored a majority of our goals from set-pieces and we spent an enormous amount of time on this area every Friday. It was an all-round system of play that demanded maximum fitness and effort from the players. If we failed or dropped below one hundred per cent the Wilkinson way collapsed. He knew that and, at the start, his methods made sure we fired on all cylinders.

The closest we came to winning something for Howard in that first season came in the Milk Cup, now the Littlewoods Trophy. After beating Huddersfield, Fulham and Luton we were drawn against Chelsea at Stamford Bridge in the quarter-final. We drew 1-1 in London and produced some brilliant first-half football in the replay to lead 3-0 in front of our own fans.

The mood in the dressing-room was one of extreme confidence. How could it have been any different? Not one person at Hillsborough that night could have envisaged the drama of the next 45 minutes. But a player called Paul Cannoville stepped into our lives and the Milk Cup was never the same again. Cannoville inspired Chelsea to come back from the dead and the score went from 3-0 to us to 4-3 to them without any of the players being able to do a thing about it. At 3-1 and 3-2 I still expected to go through but the sheer panic that set in is something I have never experienced before, or indeed after, that game. The TV recording catches a shot of Howard, eyes glazed and staring into the night in sheer disbelief. The disbelief that one of his sides could throw away a 3-0 lead and the chance of a semi-final place.

The final twist came with their full-back Doug Rougvie giving away a penalty and Mel Sterland thumping in the spot kick to take the extraordinary tie back to London. The damage was done, however − three people even died of heart attack in the midst of the excitement. We lost the second replay 2-1 and that was no real surprise after what we had gone through at Hillsborough.

It left me asking the question: "Will I ever win anything?" After going so close to promotion with Hull I was now being pulled back from a certain cup semi-final by what can only be described as one of the freak results of the Eighties.

It was, though, another typical result in our Jekyll and Hyde season. At Christmas we were going like a train. We drew at home to Villa on Boxing Day, won 3-0 at Southampton on the 29th and then on New Year's Day won at Old Trafford after another piece of Wilkinson man-management that had to be seen to be believed. We were heading for Manchester across the Pennines on a particularly cold morning, with the wind biting into your face the moment you exposed it to the conditions. On top of the Pennines Howard ordered the coach to stop and gave the instruction: "OK, we are getting out." None of us wore overcoats and we all thought he was joking. Howard, though, was deadly serious and led his team up to the top of the hill, mixing with sheep, slipping on wet grass and climbing over stiles and wire fences. It was his way of toughening up for a battle royal and, sure enough, it worked. In front of 47,638 fans we beat Manchester United 2-1. I still don't believe the build-up to that famous victory.

The more Howard pulled off strokes like that the more we believed in his methods. It was hard sometimes to keep pace with the mental and physical demands and what promised to be a superb season did tail off towards the end. Not once were we out of the top nine and that is a great performance for a newly promoted club, and yet I felt that we could have done better. Had the training been too tough? Did it make us jaded towards the end of the season when so many things are sorted out? Who knows? But the fact that we finished eighth made it a 'nearly season' for me. It definitely got tougher in the second half of the season and after that famous victory over United we only won three more matches until the end of March!

Howard kept pumping us up and mixing aggression with the caring side of his nature. He was once so concerned about the weight that Mel Sterland was putting on that he invited Mel's wife into the club to go through what Mrs Sterland was feeding her husband. He was concerned with the finest of details. He was the teacher and you were definitely the pupil.

I like to think I grew in stature that season and earned the respect of opponents, team-mates and people in the game. I played in 51 matches, scoring 12 goals in the three major competitions. It was a learning season in more ways than one and I also had my first bad experience on the field. It came after a tragic accident involving me and Everton's Adrian Heath when we drew 1-1 at Goodison Park on 1 December.

Heath and his partner Graeme Sharp were one of the best strike parterships in the game and were really buzzing at this stage in their careers. I am not a tackler and when Adrian and I went for a 50/50 ball I slid in. We made contact together but he went down badly and suffered severe torn knee ligaments. Heath was such a favourite with the Everton fans that I was immediately turned into the bad boy.

I certainly didn't mean to harm Heath. I have never tackled with malice in my life and I was grateful to Adrian and the then Everton manager Howard Kendall for exonerating me from any blame after the game, and then again on Monday morning after a video of the incident had been studied. The irony was that I too, was injured in that game when I was carried off with damaged ankle ligaments after a 'tackle' and there was no sympathy from many Evertonians.

It was, however, another first for me, an introduction to the harsh realities of the big time, and with the incident came the publicity. The position became very sad when I started to receive hate mail from Merseyside. Fortunately, Adrian and I now get on well and I respected Kendall for speaking out for me.

I was out for a couple of weeks with my ankle ligament injury while Heath didn't play again that season. It was my first real knock back in the professional game and the Heath incident played on my mind for a long time and affected me as a player. When Everton came to Hillsborough in May and beat us 1-0 I didn't get into the game and could only blame what happened at Goodison six months earlier. Howard saw what was going on and pulled me aside afterwards to give me some harsh advice. "If you are going to get on in this game," he said, "you are going to have to brush aside those kind of incidents and not be hurt by them. It's up to you."

Once again Wilkinson was right. I had learned a lesson and it was up to me to respond and become even tougher mentally.

Chapter Four

FROM HILLSBOROUGH
TO HIGHBURY

SHEFFIELD WEDNESDAY were learning to live with a hate campaign from the media. They didn't like us or the way we played and they made it known. Howard was the main butt of their criticism. There was no way that he was going to win them over and I believe that the stinging attacks on him and his beliefs simply made him even more determined to succeed. "I'll do it my way and we'll go one better this season" was his attitude as we prepared for the 1985-86 season.

New squad players were introduced like Gary Thompson, a coloured centre forward with an exciting reputation, Mark Chamberlain, a gifted winger who was on the verge of breaking through with England, Simon Stainrod, a player with enormous skill but with a suspect temperament, and Ziggi Jonsson, a midfield star from Iceland who had been watched by many First Division clubs. There was power in the new signings but skill too and it seemed that Howard was giving himself the option of changing tactics if he had to. Stainrod was a typical Wilkinson signing – Howard enjoyed taking players who had lost their way and turning them into winners. He liked his staff to feel grateful and there is no question that he felt that he had the 'Midas' touch.

The pre-season was just the same and this was no surprise because the Sheffield Wednesday professionals are sent on their summer breaks with a strict training schedule. Howard believes in total commitment 24 hours a day, 12 months a year and even on holiday he likes you to be careful and watch what you eat. Summers away from Hillsborough are spent on long runs and the players tested the moment they report back for pre-season training.

Howard toyed with changing the system and for a few matches in pre-season we switched to a 4-4-2 formation. But it was never the Wednesday way and we were back playing three up front and hitting long balls before the season kicked off.

The manager had lost none of his enthusiasm and once again the players responded. We were in the top three by mid-September and became the club to end Manchester United's amazing 15-match unbeaten run under Ron Atkinson. The signs were good that Wilkinson's hard work and undying devotion would be rewarded with a prize.

I learned a lesson the hard way after the United victory. I told a press man, Vince Wilson of the *Sunday Mirror*, that we were not surprised at our victory and that the lads had even had a few bob on ourselves to beat United. The next morning what I thought was a private conversation was splashed all over the papers and I had discovered when and where to keep my mouth shut. The Football Association were even involved and I couldn't believe how naïve I had been.

There was a set-back to our impressive start when Everton thrashed us 5-1 at home and we lost by the same margin at Tottenham. He was determined to get his own back in February when they visited Hillsborough on a freezing Saturday afternoon. The match could easily have been called off but Howard ordered the ground staff to work around the clock to keep the game on. He said that they wouldn't fancy it, wound us up in the dressing-room, told us to hit it long and get at them . . . and was then dismayed when Spurs completed the double by winning 2-1!

It didn't deter him for long and every minute, every day, he worked at building Hillsborough into a formidable fortress. He had seen the late, great Bill Shankly do it at Anfield for Liverpool and he wanted the same respect for his Wednesday club.

There was bitter disappointment again when we lost to Everton in the semi-final of the FA Cup. We had played so well in beating West Brom, Orient, Derby and West Ham and then just couldn't go that one extra step. That was beginning to haunt Howard Wilkinson and his team. Everton beat us at Villa Park 2-1 and the atmosphere in the dressing-room was one of "Not again!" It was also the third time in my career that I had been close to glory and, yes, I began to doubt my own way into the record books.

If I thought I was disappointed about the Cup, it only brought back memories of bitter disappointment when England manager Bobby Robson put me on standby for a friendly International in Egypt in January, only to overlook me when first choice wingers John Barnes and Chris Waddle both dropped out. He called up Danny Wallace of Southampton instead and salt was rubbed into the wound when Wallace started the game and scored on his debut.

I thought I was a must when Barnes and Waddle were forced to drop out with injury. I had been playing well, scoring goals in the First Division consistently and, with Howard seemingly close to Robson and the Football Association, I thought I must make it. The call never came, despite the fact that I literally slept on the phone for 24 hours. (You have heard the phrase "wait by the phone", well, that was me.) It took me a long time to get over that snub. My feeling was that if I didn't break into the England set-up now, I never would.

My England call never came and the season ended with Sheffield Wednesday finishing in fifth position, a three-place improvement on the previous year. I was delighted to end as top scorer in the League with 13 goals, including three penalties. I have always been happy to take penalties and, with Mel Sterland just as confident, there was no shortage of volunteers when the decisions went our way. I got 15 goals in all that season and was happy with that return.

Fifth place and the semi-final, however, wasn't good enough for the club or a manager with the high ambitions of Howard. He needed to be a winner and I couldn't help wondering after two full seasons at Hillsborough whether he would succeed with this club. Were Wednesday big enough for him? Only time would tell.

The 1986-87 season was a vital one for Wilkinson and the team he had built. We had finished eighth and fifth in the League and gone close in two cup competitions. Everyone knew we had to improve to continue the momentum of a club who were desperate for success. Would the players keep responding to Howard's Way of coaching, would the strain be too much on us, would his fear factor fall on deaf ears this time after the team hadn't experienced it for so long? These were all vital questions that had to be answered. I must admit that I had my doubts whether we could better fifth and the semi-final of the FA Cup. It was a tall order for any club in the land.

Once again Howard thought about changing the system that had brought so much reward. It was as if he knew Wednesday had to change to go forward, but he did it without conviction. I am not sure whether or not he believed we had the players to revert to an orthodox 4-4-2 system, or was it that the players had become Wilkinson clones and couldn't change?

Mark Chamberlain, who had not really been used before, was now introduced as an out-and-out right-winger and I was ordered to stay wide on the left. It was not a role I particularly relished and I approached the season with a certain amount of reluctance. I was disappointed to be switched from the free role I had played in for so long.

We started with Chappie and Carl Shutt up front and Mark and I playing wide and, amazingly, it worked well. We only lost one of our first nine matches and found ourselves in a similar position, nestling just in the top five. Then we lost at United, drew at Spurs when we should have won, and lost at Forest. Wilkinson switched back to the long ball and a three-man attack. It suited me but it showed us that the manager had no real confidence in getting results without using the tactics he had drilled into the players.

Lee Chapman was scoring regularly and there was tremendous pressure on him because goals were hard to come by in the rest of the side. David Hirst came in from Barnsley and had a lot of raw talent but he found the step up difficult to take. Perhaps, like me at first, he found the training intimidating and the physical and mental pressure a torture.

We were still in the top ten at Christmas only to fall away badly in the second half of the season. We didn't win a game in 1987 until 21 March. It wasn't good enough and the slump wasn't helped when we went out of the FA Cup in the quarter-final at Hillsborough to Coventry. They went on to beat Spurs in a great final but that didn't help us or the mood of the fans.

After four years at Hillsborough Wilkinson was being closely examined. The media had always been against him and his methods and now the supporters were beginning to ask questions. Like all football fans, the manager is popular when things go well and the culprit when results are poor. They began to give Howard some stick.

At one stage, on 18 April when we lost at Norwich, we had nosedived into 17th place and looked like relegation candidates. Fortunately we recovered, beat QPR at home 7-1 and stayed up, finishing in 13th place. Relegation would have been bitterly disappointing and not what Howard deserved after putting so much into the club.

Howard, though, had never been a great communicator with the supporters and this went against him when we started to slide. The supporters couldn't relate to him, couldn't understand him and he was an obvious butt for their frustration. It was the first time that things started to go wrong for Howard at Hillsborough and he knew he had to plug the gap – or else. It was, sadly, a struggle from that season on.

I only got six goals, including four penalties and although I suffered with injury it was particularly disappointing for me. A measure of the pressure on Lee Chapman was the fact that he was top scorer with 19 goals and next came Carl Shutt, with just seven.

It was all disappointing and frustrating and my own feeling towards the club hadn't been helped when in March I was linked with Arsenal. I first discovered Arsenal's interest through a newspaper report when it was claimed that Arsenal's new manager George Graham had started a £3 million manhunt and I was on his hit list. There is no question that I found being linked with one of the top five clubs in the country difficult to handle and it certainly played on my mind for the rest of the season. I asked Howard about the interest but he said that he had not heard anything from Graham. I had no option but to take his word for it. If the story was true I knew deep down that I would want to join Arsenal because Sheffield Wednesday are a powerful club, but Arsenal are one of the élite and any footballer worth his salt wants to play for the best.

I spoke to Howard many times about the future in the summer of 1987. I knew that he was reaching a crossroads of his career at Hillsborough and he had told the board of directors that he needed money to use in the transfer market to take Sheffield Wednesday on to the next stage of his plans. He knew that if he wasn't given cash to strengthen the side then there was no way that Wednesday would be good enough to improve on what he had already achieved.

He was persuasive and tempted me with a new improved contract that was to keep me at Hillsborough at least until 1990. The deal made me the highest-paid player on the books and it certainly gave me a boost. There were fringe benefits to the contract that appealed to me, like the pension scheme, loyalty bonuses, a company car and other perks. I also liked living in Sheffield and my role in the side, and while a lot of players were taking advantage of the freedom of contract system and moving as free agents at the end of their agreements, I was happy to sign and stay.

Howard had assured me that he had not heard a thing from Arsenal and there was no other decision for me than to sign the contract. I hoped that the club would follow my loyalty and the enthusiasm of Howard and back him with money for new players. Sadly new faces didn't arrive and the new season began disastrously. I felt sorry for Howard because

In the Mood for Arsenal

by not backing him in the transfer market the club seemed to be admitting that they were happy to sit in behind the big boys – the winners.

Wednesday were not helped by a crippling list of injuries and it was an extremely inexperienced side which began the season with a 2-1 defeat at Chelsea. In our second game, at home to Oxford, my old Hull mate, Billy Whitehurst, put me out of the game for two months with a bad tackle that tore knee ligaments. Billy was understandably upset and yet these things happen – they are part and parcel of football. Like my challenge on Adrian Heath, there was no malice meant.

The results were poor and we were pinned in the bottom group for the first half of the season, not winning our first match until a 2-0 home victory over Charlton on 26 September. There was tremendous pressure on Howard at this stage. The fans were against him and even an action group sprung up, headed by a man named Michael Deakin, who wanted to get on the board and run the club.

It was harsh reality for the manager and the players. Had we come as far as we could together? The impact of his shock treatment was certainly not the same. When the cups hit the wall at half-time it was a question of thinking "Howard is throwing those cups again" rather than being shocked and stimulated into greater effort. I began to wonder if, like Hull, I had reached the point when a new club would do me good.

I'd signed a new contract and had tremendous loyalty towards Wednesday but it seemed as if the club had not backed Howard and things were running out of control. The honeymoon was over and the first rows were cropping up. It wasn't working. To play Howard's way the players had to have a steel edge to their game, there had to be passion, commitment and an up-and-at-them approach. The rollickings were not having that effect on us any more. We were not jumping when he tore into us.

When I returned from my knee injury the rumours about Arsenal were alive again. There was also talk of Aberdeen, Celtic and even Spurs and, yes, I was unsettled. Howard kept telling me that there was nothing going on but I couldn't

Happier days with George, or is he trying to strangle me?

believe that there was no smoke without fire. The fans, upset
and unsettled by the continuous rumours, began to turn on
me. It was frustration for me because I had done nothing to
trigger off transfer talk and had signed my new contract in
good faith.

As the results dropped and the speculation increased I have
to admit that I began to lose my enthusiasm for the club. I
wasn't playing well but Wednesday were not having the same
effect on me. I was not gripped by the thought of going out
to die for the cause.

This period, around Christmas 1987, was the most unsettling
of my career. I had been injured, was struggling for form and
the Arsenal business got me down. It seemed that everyone
knew about it but nothing happened. At last Howard admitted
that George Graham had asked about me without making any
firm bid. A couple of days later it was reported that Arsenal had
had a £500,000 offer turned down! I was never told whether
that was true.

It was Peter Eustace who actually let the cat out of the bag
without even realising it. He once growled at me: "You don't

want to go to Arsenal, I had terrible problems when I once went to London and played for West Ham. You are a big fish in a small pond here, you'll get eaten up there." It was as if I was going and yet I had not been told anything. The manager said there had been no bid, while his assistant was advising me not to sign for Arsenal.

I discovered after joining Arsenal that offers were made and that George Graham had tried for months to sign me. I still don't know why Howard didn't want me to know that. It would have been easy to say "Yes, we have had a bid but you are under contract and there is no way you are going."

All any professional footballer asks from his manager is honesty. I had given the club good service and was disappointed with the way they treated me. I thought they should have come clean and given me the option of discussing things with Wilkinson and my family.

Sheffield Wednesday didn't officially admit Arsenal's interest until Tuesday 22 March. My Hillsborough career had reached an all-time low the previous Saturday when I was named as sub for a home game against Portsmouth and Howard spent 20 minutes after the game having a go at me. I was due to play for the reserves on the Tuesday but was suddenly pulled out of the game in the morning with the instruction instead to go to Hillsborough and see the manager.

I knew what was coming. It had to be. Howard didn't stand on ceremony when I walked into his office. He just said: "Son, I have given permission for you to speak to Arsenal and you are meeting George Graham tonight at eight o'clock on the motorway at Sandyacre."

Just like that. After a year of being linked with them, I was now being told that I could talk to Arsenal. I felt strange. It was a mixture of relief to hear from the horse's mouth and yet I felt sad that after four years it should end with barriers up between Howard and myself. I wanted to say thanks and shake Howard by the hand and admit that it had been great. I wanted to say that I had never met a manager like him before and that I would never forget the experience, but the right words just didn't come out. We had grown apart and it was a sad way to end.

There is no question that I had experienced great times at Hillsborough and as I stood in front of Wilkinson I thought back over the last four years. It had been hard but the rewards had been good. Wilkinson had plucked me from obscurity at Hull and put me on the next rung of the ladder. He had got the best out of me his way and now, when I was 28 years old, he was offering me the biggest transfer of most footballers' lives. I had not even met George Graham or put pen to paper but it was accepted that I would be on my way.

Howard Wilkinson knew, and so did I, that it was time for Brian Marwood to part company with Sheffield Wednesday. I drove home and told Lesley, "We are going to sign for Arsenal."

Chapter Five
SUCCESS BEFORE CASH

NOTHING WAS going to stop me signing for Arsenal.

Not even the disappointment that George Graham wanted me to play wide on the left, a position I didn't favour. "I can see you either playing wide on the left, down the right or through the middle", he said but there was no free role for me at Highbury.

Not even the fact that I signed for Arsenal for the same basic wage I was receiving at Hillsborough, and talk of players at Highbury earning £2,000 a week basic is just not true. However, I considered that the bonuses I could receive if Arsenal maintained their success rate under Graham would fully compensate for no big salary increase.

Not even the fact that Ian Porterfield, my old Sunderland hero and at that time manager of Aberdeen, wanted to sign me again.

No, it had to be Arsenal. Professional footballers want to play at the top for the best clubs and this was my chance. A coach at Hull once told me to always go with your hunch in life and my hunch was sign for Arsenal.

George Graham was just coming to the end of his second season in control and the signs were that he was building Arsenal into a formidable force again in football. They had won the Littlewoods Cup the previous season and had got through to Wembley again to defend their trophy. So when I met Graham that night at a hotel at Sandyacre I had no doubts that I would sign for him, even before talks opened.

George was on his way to watch the England Under-21 side take on Scotland and he made it clear as soon as we met that he wanted to keep our meeting and the possibility of me signing for Arsenal a secret until the deal had been completed. It was strange therefore to be talking at a hotel swarming with players and coaches en route to games in that area of the country.

We talked about Arsenal, my role in the side, his ambitions, my own dreams, money, and it was agreed that I would travel to London the following morning and complete the deal. As I drove home I looked upon the dream move as a transfer to put me out of my misery, and it was extremely depressing to think of Sheffield Wednesday like that after so many happy times.

I had to go back to Hillsborough to collect my boots and it was a sad and emotional moment for me because I had become close to a lot of people. I knew the washerwomen and groundsman like old friends and I wanted to say goodbye to them all. Howard and I met face to face for the last time and once again it was difficult to say the things that expressed my true feelings. Deep down I knew I had respect for the man and yet something held me back from telling him how much I appreciated what he had done for me. The words didn't come easily to him either and he just said that George Graham was getting a bargain at £600,000. He wished me all the best and that was that, the end of an era.

I didn't sleep the night before I travelled down to London to complete the Arsenal deal and I was in good time to get

Happy days with Arsenal. I sign for Arsenal and George Graham welcomes me to Highbury.

the Sheffield train to Kings Cross. I journeyed without an advisor and agent although I knew that I could contact an old friend, Nigel Early, who is an expert in contracts and agreements, if any problems arose. I had also related the basic wage figure I was going to receive to Gordon Taylor and he had told me that it matched up to most of the figures in the First Division.

There were no obstacles from Arsenal. Once again I discussed things with George Graham and the financial package was outlined by Ken Friar, the club's chief executive. He explained how much money would be paid by the club into a pension scheme and that there would be loyalty bonuses and, of course, the bonuses for success. That was the key for me and I fully expected to enjoy big rewards. Playing for Arsenal would also open promotional doors, although the one thing that did surprise me was that there was no club company car contract, a facility I had enjoyed at Sheffield. It would mean the extra expense of

So this is Highbury.

buying my own car and, of course, the London property market scared me to death. Our home in Sheffield cost £50,000 while the houses I had seen in suitable positions close to Arsenal's training ground at London Colney were five times that figure. Since we moved down and into our new house my mortgage repayments have increased by £600 a month and that just proves the difference in the standard of living across the country. All I can say is thank God for bonuses but there is no question that I am worse off since playing in London.

I have never regretted the move, however, and I would have always kicked myself if I had backed away from the transfer for financial reasons. I have said before that money has not been a critical motivation in my career and so, on 23 March 1988, and at 28 years old, I signed for Arsenal in a £600,000 deal. As soon as I put pen to paper I felt good. Again, it was the next rung of the ladder. I didn't realise that there were shocks in store and the first was to come even before I had set foot outside Highbury.

The commando-type training that I had flogged through for so long at Sheffield had taken its toll. The road running for days and weeks on end had resulted in an achilles heel problem and Arsenal's club doctor Len Sash explained to me that one achilles was bigger than the other. I could see that he was getting cold feet on the deal and panic struck in. I thought: "Oh no, so close and yet so far." I believed that Arsenal were going to back out of the deal.

The man who came to my rescue was Arsenal's physio Gary Lewin, whom I had spoken with about all the road running I had experienced at Sheffield. Lewin helped persuade the club that there were no major problems, although I signed with Arsenal accepting that one day I would probably need an achilles operation.

I signed a straight three-year contract, a deal that would take me to the age of 31 and I was happy with that. Perhaps then, when possibly the last contract of my career would have to be negotiated, would I put money before ambition.

Then came a very prickly press conference. The general attitude of the London journalists asking the question like

"Brian Who?" and when John Etheridge, from the *Sun* newspaper asked me if I thought £600,000 was a lot for a 28-year-old I vowed that by the time I had finished my contract the whole country would have heard of me. The sniping hurt because I was proud of my record in football and the fact that I had fought my way to the top from nowhere.

Nothing was going to spoil this move. I had got back the excitement that had been missing over the last few months at Hillsborough, that tingle of expectancy that goes with playing for a big club. I knew I was doing the right thing.

By the time I got home at seven o'clock I was totally exhausted. It had been a long day and at that stage no one knew that Lesley and I were also going through an emotional and worrying time with our second daughter Sophie, who had been born ten days before I signed for Arsenal. Sophie, alas, was born with a hip problem – 'clicky hips' following a breech birth. Her hips were dislocated and it wasn't long before a doctor confirmed that she would have to go into a harness, with her legs in plaster and bent up to her chest. It was upsetting to say the least and particularly traumatic for Lesley.

You can imagine the scene. The husband is away and living in a hotel while he tries to settle into a new club, while the wife is left alone to look after the home, cope with the worries of a newly born daughter, mother year-old Charlotte and also try and organise our move from Sheffield.

It was a period that we can now look back on and wonder how we got through it. It was a period of pressure and problems and it led to many phone calls between us from opposite ends of the country, when we said the wrong things to each other. It was pure frustration and it often led to us arguing about trivial things.

Arsenal were fantastic throughout the problem days. The boss couldn't have been more helpful and he allowed me to go home whenever it was possible, often giving me unscheduled days off if Sophie had a hospital appointment.

I was also helped in a strange sort of way by the fact that I was cup-tied and couldn't play in the Littlewoods Cup at Wembley. It meant that the boss was not under pressure to play me as he stuck with his final formation. I had been cup-tied, ironically against Arsenal, in the only match I played that season in the competition. Arsenal beat us 1-0 in a quarter-final at Hillsborough in January when poor Martin Hodge let a long shot by Nigel Winterburn slip in through his hands and legs and over the line.

My domestic pressure was unexpectedly increased again when I made my debut at Oxford late in March and pulled a thigh muscle in the second half. The injury was a blow professionally because I wanted to establish myself with my new club and had begun to form a good relationship with left-back Kenny Sansom. However, the injury kept me out for a month and it allowed me even more time to spend with Lesley and the girls.

Poor little Sophie was kept in a harness for two months but it became impossible when she started to bring food up because of the pressure on her stomach. It was a time in our lives filled with worry and she needed a lot of monitoring. She wasn't crawling and there were continuous check-ups until we visited a Great Ormond Street specialist who, at last, gave us hope for the future. He decided that she didn't need an operation and insisted that she would improve daily. That diagnosis has been proved spot on and today Sophie is a happy, normal girl who runs in and out of the home causing the normal chaos. It is difficult to describe the relief and happiness that Lesley and I have experienced seeing her recover and our attitude has often been: "As long as she can walk, that's OK." There still have to be hospital checks but it has been a full recovery.

The stress of a disrupted family life probably cost us £9,000 on our move from Sheffield. The house was on the market for £85,000 and we had seen a home in Wheathamstead that we didn't want to lose. At the last minute our buyer dropped out and a lady who worked for the estate agents who were handling the deal repeated an earlier offer of £76,000 from herself. Lesley had had enough, the family needed to be together and we accepted the offer and waved away £9,000, which must have made that lady in the estate agents very happy – or shrewd.

Arsenal lost the Littlewoods Cup final to Luton in extra time. It was an exciting game with us coming from behind only to lose it in the last seconds. Nigel also missed a penalty. The reception afterwards, organised in an Italian restaurant by Graham Rix, was a sombre affair until a few drinks relaxed everyone. It was certainly a chance for me to mix socially with the players for the first time. In Sheffield social gatherings and players' nights out are far more frequent than in London.

My next game for Arsenal was, ironically, at Hillsborough when we drew 3-3 with Sheffield Wednesday. It was strange to go back so quickly and it was a remarkable game with us equalising in the last few minutes. I didn't play particularly well and got a roasting from George Graham after the match for roaming from my position wide on the left. Old habits die hard!

The following week I scored from the penalty spot on my home debut against Coventry in a 1-1 draw. Arsenal had a bad track record of missing penalties, including Nigel's Wembley mistake and other misses by Kenny, Michael Thomas and Martin Hayes. I volunteered to try and end the jinx. I had always been confident of scoring from 12 yards. Howard had given me the tip of running from a long way to take them. His attitude was that if you only stroll up to the spot there is no momentum.

The club finished sixth in that 1987-88 season and I believe that George Graham realised that changes had to be made to turn Arsenal into a side that would take him on to the next development in his plans. Graham Rix, Charlie Nicholas and Kenny Sansom were all players he decided had come to the end of their careers at Highbury. It was time to break up the squad.

There is a lot of Howard Wilkinson in George Graham. They are both down-to-earth managers with no grey areas. It is either black or white with both men. A difference is that George is not so intense and allows himself days off to relax away from the club while Howard was seven days a week, 24 hours a day Sheffield Wednesday.

George also had Theo Foley, a bubbly Irishman who helped take the pressure off in the dressing-room and with the players. Theo was the funny guy while George was the straight character and very much the boss. Howard didn't have that kind of relationship with his staff. They were all straight guys who wanted you to work and not have fun.

You never see George acting the clown, being jovial or jolly because that is not his public image. He is a shrewd, thorough manager who wants to be a winner. There is a distinct feeling when you are talking to George Graham that he knows exactly where he is going. It is all plotted out in his brain and you shouldn't try and stand in his way.

When I signed for Arsenal I put ambition before money because I felt that success would not be far away . . . but not even I dreamed how quickly it would happen.

Chapter Six
CHAMPIONS

EVERYONE ON the Arsenal bench held his breath.

We were packed tight down on the touchline at Anfield, all squashed together in the little visitors' box which had witnessed so much misery and disappointment for so many. There was George, Theo, physio Gary Lewin, scout Steve Burtenshaw, youth team coach Stewart Houston, subs Perry Groves, Martin Hayes and me.

I had made up my mind that on this night I was going to be on the bench. There was no way I wanted to be pushed up into the stand, not on this night, Friday 26 May 1989 and the climax of the 1988-89 Championship race. It was the biggest night for years, easily the biggest match I had been involved in and despite the achilles heel operation that was still stitched up I wanted to be directly involved with the action, the emotion and the excitement as Arsenal chased a 2-0 victory to win the title. To do it at Anfield against the favourites and the most powerful team in the land was unheard of.

But there, in the last seconds, was Michael Thomas,

The goal I will never forget. Michael Thomas wins the Championship for Arsenal with the last kick of the game of the season at arch-rivals Liverpool.

bearing down on goal. It was a sight I will never forget and for a split second no one on that Arsenal bench could believe it. There had been so much shouting and encouragement from us and yet at the crucial moment we held our breath.

Goal! Champions, chaos, tears, champagne, party time! How do you describe nine months' work packed into a split second when Thomas flicked the ball over Liverpool goalkeeper Bruce Grobbelaar for a story-book finish that no one will forget? The nation watched on television. It was the greatest climax of any season in the history of football.

Suddenly there was joy unbounded on the pitch at Anfield. The referee David Hutchinson from Oxford blew the final whistle and the Arsenal people, fans, staff, directors were engulfed as one big happy family. I jumped so high at the end I felt that I had popped the stitches in my heel.

The rest of the night was just a blur of pleasure. The Championship presentation, the dressing-room, the coach, the night club, the morning after. Who cares about hangovers

The celebrations begin. Thomas's expression tells the story and Nigel Winterburn joins the fun.

when you have got a Championship medal? And, at last, you are a winner.

The Championship in my first full season at Highbury – who would have thought that it would have ended like this? Saturday, 27 August 1988, at Wimbledon when we kicked off to Friday, 26 May 1989, at Anfield is a long road to journey. There were a few potholes and punctures along the way – but we made it. It is good now to reflect on the kind of season I dreamed of when I was a kid all those years ago at Hull.

I had only played three and a half games for Arsenal and needed a pre-season boost before the opening of the 1988-89 season, and I got it at, of all places, Wembley. Arsenal were involved in a tournament against Spurs, Liverpool and Bayern Munich and I notched two goals as we ripped our North London rivals apart in the first game. It was a great moment for me because, apart from the fact that I had

The Championship trophy, held aloft by skipper Tony Adams with John Lukic and Lee Dixon making sure he doesn't drop it.

never played at Wembley before, the goals allowed the fans to discover just who Brian Marwood is.

We beat Bayern Munich 3-0 in the final and the performance and victory was just an extension of the good form we had shown in our pre-season build-up. We didn't lose a game on our Sweden tour and returned home to prove to our supporters that we meant business. It is easy to say so now but before a ball was kicked the players felt that it could just be a special year. I scored five goals and felt part of the Arsenal set-up for the first time.

I had approached the training when we reported back after the summer break with a great deal of trepidation following my experiences at Sheffield. Fortunately Arsenal's training was more interesting, involving a great deal of ball work.

The first four days were spent at Trent Park in Cockfosters with a breaking-in programme of runs and stamina work. It was a gradual build-up and the switch to the training headquarters at London Colney brought more running but also the introduction of ball work and skills.

The build-up to matches began on tour and followed with friendlies against Leicester and Birmingham. By the end the training, I'm certain, was just as physically demanding although it passed quicker and was more enjoyable because of the different venues and working programmes. It wasn't running, running and more running.

Liverpool, understandably, were the bookmakers' favourites and we had been put in second place because of our good pre-season form. There was no question that there was a lot of confidence in the side and that helped some of the new faces like Steve Bould and Lee Dixon from Stoke and Paul Merson, the striker who was emerging from the youth policy at Highbury.

When we went to Wimbledon for the big kick-off we couldn't see anything but winning despite Wimbledon's reputation as a battling side with the habit of spoiling the best laid plans. It was the perfect start, with Alan Smith getting a hat-trick and Merson and I supplying the other goals in a superb 5-1 victory. I was delighted with my goal and it was the start of a little run of scoring in the first six matches,

One of my first goals for Arsenal, against North London rivals Spurs at Wembley in a pre-season tournament.

including a 3-2 victory at Spurs. The only disappointment in those early weeks was our home form. We lost to Aston Villa and then drew 2-2 against Southampton after being 2-0 down at half-time.

It was the match against Southampton that galvanised Arsenal into the headlines again, but for all the wrong reasons. The now infamous Paul Davis incident when Paul broke Glen Cockerill's jaw with a left hook took everyone by surprise and no one at Highbury that day, not the referee, both managers, linesmen or the players knew what had really gone on.

Southampton's Russell Osman had mentioned something on the pitch to me about seeing Paul Davis throw a punch but it was said without conviction and there was certainly no stoppage because of anything illegal. Unfortunately for Paul, or fortunately for football, news cameras on ITV were

77

covering the game, and picked up the punch and highlighted it on London Weekend Television that Saturday night. That blew the story sky high and it resulted in one of the biggest controversies to hit football. It ended with Paul receiving a record nine-match ban from the Football Association.

After the game there was no real mention of what had happened, for the simple reason that not one Arsenal player had seen Davis throw the punch. Paul certainly didn't offer an explanation or even talk about any incident with Cockerill.

The facts now are simple. Paul retaliated off the ball after being the victim of a lot of intimidation. There had been a lot of things going on in the game surrounding Davis and Cockerill and I have to say the Southampton player was not entirely innocent. But if I have to put my hand on my heart, and I am not talking now as an Arsenal footballer or a member of the PFA management committee, but as someone who loves the game, I have to say that the television people were right to show the incident. Whatever the reasons for the retaliation, Paul was wrong. Those things have to be stamped out of the game and he had to pay the penalty. Television has put a lot of money into the sport and they had a right to be at the match. Having scooped the rest of the media, they also had every right to show the pictures.

What I don't agree with is the inconsistency of football in dealing with such cases. Television was used to condemn Paul Davis and yet on other occasions the FA refuses to accept television footage. Later in the season Mark Ward, then playing for West Ham, was sent off at Charlton when he clearly didn't touch Colin Pates, now an Arsenal player. Television pictures proved Ward's innocence and could have cleared him but the FA refused and went ahead and gave Ward a suspension. That is definitely wrong.

I realised that the Davis incident was serious for him and the club as soon as I heard that it had been on the television news, and then when I read the Monday papers. . . . It dominated every sports page and I felt sorry for Davis on Monday morning at training. He is a sensitive lad and got wickedly baited, football-style, with comments such as "Here comes Mike Tyson" or a nickname of "The Boxer".

In my England strip and it looks as though Bobby Robson has made me a one-cap wonder.

George tried to play the whole affair down in a clear effort to keep the pressure off his players but as the days went on Paul began to become affected by it. Davis, ironically, was the club's PFA representative, and that led to a series of problems with the players union. Paul wanted backing but we felt that the PFA couldn't support that kind of behaviour and Davis, feeling hard done by, resigned.

No one blamed him for that because he was in an impossible situation. He was charged by the FA with bringing the game into disrepute and the publicity and the possibility of a fine definitely affected him as a player and person. Everyone expected him to be suspended, but not for nine matches. When the players heard the official verdict we were shocked and stunned. It was like a bombshell for the club.

Paul Davis, of course, regrets his moment of madness. In a split second he put his name in the record books for the wrong reasons and put a blossoming England career on ice. The players tried to make light of it and yet we knew the damage had been done.

Arsenal don't make a big exhibition of behaviour because they expect players to act on and off the field like mature adults. I have only been sent off once in my career, when playing for Hull against Sheffield United in the middle of a referees' crackdown on reckless tackles. Everyone knows that I couldn't tackle a fish and chip supper let alone a defender but I got the red card for two clumsy challenges on United full-back Mick Henderson. The referee came over to talk to me and with the crowd baying for my dismissal he told me "You're going, son". I couldn't believe it. I couldn't speak to anyone, didn't feel like eating, refused to tell my parents and even cried myself to sleep. I thought I had disgraced my family, Hull and myself and it was a long time before I got over the shock.

It was not as though I had committed a bad foul by going through the defender and it makes me laugh to think of my sending-off when I see what goes on today. The sending-off, however, remains a blot on my copy book and I can appreciate what Paul Davis went through over the

Cockerill affair. My offence was minor by comparison and yet it allowed me to understand and try and help him in any way I could.

Arsenal, meanwhile, had to carry on picking up points to stabilise the ship and maintain our good early-season form. We lost at Sheffield Wednesday, thrashed West Ham at Upton Park and moved into second place after beating Coventry 2-0 at Highbury. I was scoring goals, was happy with my form and there was even speculation that I might be called up for England.

I had been close to the national squad before, against Egypt, and didn't want to dream too much even though I knew I was playing some of the best football of my career. In September I had the heartbreak of having to drop out of the squad to play at home to Denmark and then it happened, Bobby Robson picked me for the party for a friendly International in Saudi Arabia. There were five of us in the pool, skipper Tony Adams, Alan Smith, David Rocastle, Michael Thomas and me, and it reflected how well the Arsenal side was playing.

It was a dream come true, a fairytale, especially at 28 years old, and I couldn't believe it when our chief scout, Steve Burtenshaw, came into the dressing-room and read out the names who had been picked for England. Then I was convinced I would play.

The press seemed to be on my side and indicated in the build-up to the game that I would start. There had been no real indication from the manager and yet I am a great believer that there is no smoke without fire. John Barnes of Liverpool was injured and that meant that Chris Waddle and I were the only wingers in the party flying to the other side of the world. It was a friendly International and the perfect opportunity for Robson to experiment and have a look at new faces like Paul Gascoigne and me. He knew all about Waddle and Peter Beardsley. They were established Internationals with almost one hundred caps between them. I thought about the game a lot and the more I considered his options the more confident I grew of starting the match.

Arsenal's last game before Saudi was away to Newcastle

and their defender Andy Thorn almost put me out of the International with a ghastly over the top tackle that jarred my groin. I thought, "Oh no, not again", only for the knock to clear up and finally disappear after some after-match treatment.

England flew out on Concorde, a prestige flight and reward for their association with British Airways. The manager welcomed all the new faces and I was stimulated just to be with the best players in the land and talk new ideas with fresh faces.

On the Monday I was still convinced that I would play. Twenty-four hours later I was gutted after being left out of the team and stuck on the bench with the rest of the squad. There was only Tony Dorigo of Chelsea who didn't strip for action. Michael Thomas gained his first cap, which was great, Rocky was included and so too were Mel Sterland, David Seaman and Garry Pallister. But no Brian Marwood. Bobby Robson said that he was close to playing me but he wanted to retain some experience in the side. It was small consolation to be told that he would get me involved at some stage.

The match didn't go well. Saudi Arabia took the lead and England struggled throughout to hit any real form against opposition which should have been put in their place. The longer England misfired the more I thought I might get on. I tried to catch Bobby Robson's eye a couple of times in the hope that he might be reminded that I was bursting to be given a chance.

With nine minutes left I got the nod to make my England debut. Don't get me wrong, there is no one prouder than me to play for my country, but what could I achieve in a few minutes? I got in a few crosses and from one Bryan Robson came within a hair's breadth of scoring the winner but it was all over before I realised what was happening.

There was a team meeting after the game and the manager emphasised how important it was for players to take their club form into International matches. He spoke about my crosses and said that there was no better set-piece taker in football. It gave me hope and I flew home by Concorde

Me with the Championship trophy.

expecting to be given another chance. After all no one can make up their mind about a player in just nine minutes.

I was wrong, Bobby Robson did. I have never been near an England squad since.

I will never understand to this day why he took me to Saudi Arabia and then discarded me after just nine minutes.

It was a waste of time. Why didn't he fill the place with someone he had his eye on for the long-term future? Did he do it to keep the press happy? Did he just forget about me? I don't expect I will ever know the answers. The facts remain, however, that a 28-year-old player was picked, given nine minutes and tossed aside without explanation.

Bobby Robson certainly didn't speak to me after the game, hasn't spoken to me since and has never given anyone at Arsenal an explanation. I call that bad management. You must tell players the truth and managers would gain more respect if they stuck to that principle.

It was the same when Howard told me that Arsenal had not made a bid. There is no point in lying and, yes, I felt hard done by by Robson. I still cling to the hope that one day I might get the chance to prove him wrong but the dream is rapidly disappearing. My old advice of never going through life with a regret often comes up and hits me when I think of England.

Professional footballers often suffer kicks in the teeth and here was mine. I felt that Bobby Robson let me down by dropping me with no reason. I can't even see why he picked me in the first place and I often sit and ask myself the question. I am a sensible and logical person but his actions defeated me.

I was selected for my country and never given the chance to prove what I could do. Why? Only one person knows the answer and I would like to think that if I ever became a manager I wouldn't treat any of my players like that. Had I played and done badly I would have held my hands up and conceded defeat.

It is my firm belief that Robson didn't want a winger like me who gets in crosses. He liked Barnes and Waddle and I couldn't ever see him breaking up that partnership while he was England manager. Perhaps if Alan Smith or Mark Hateley had been up front it would have been different for me. Anyway, I will just have to paste over my nine minutes and put it down to a bitter experience.

I don't know whether it was the dust storm we flew into when we arrived in Saudi or the food but I must have picked

In tune with Arsenal and the boys make a Championship record.

up a virus and it developed into a flu-type bug that laid me low for a few games. I played at Charlton and scored the two goals that put us top of the table and never felt so physically drained in my life. I sat in the dressing-room after the game and thought to myself: "You have just scored two goals, we are top and you should be celebrating." All I felt was depression and lethargy.

I played against Liverpool when they knocked us out of the Littlewoods Cup in a third-round second replay with their best performance of the season. Liverpool were brilliant that night and although we took the lead, by the end we had to admire their football and concede defeat. It was the first time that Liverpool had touched their peak and it opened up everyone's eyes to just how dangerous they were to our own Championship ambitions.

The virus was getting me down and I underwent a series of tests, took urine tablets and was told that it was just a case of plodding on and letting the pills take their course. I didn't really recover until the FA Cup third round when we drew 2-2 at West Ham in the live TV game after going

2-0 down. We expected to win the replay because West Ham had been struggling and Arsenal at home should be capable of beating anyone when it matters. We huffed and puffed, however, and Leroy Rosenior scored a late winner for them. It was a real sickener and meant that we were now out of both major cup competitions. I had learned again that the more you expect, the more you are let down.

It was vital now for us to keep winning in the League. Liverpool, who had been 14 points adrift at one stage, had started to put a run together and the media were building up the race. That helped us in a way because the fans and the critics were looking more at Liverpool catching us rather than Arsenal maintaining their position at the top. We had a great win at Everton, struggled to draw 1-1 with Sheffield Wednesday at home, took revenge on West Ham and beat Millwall at The Den but the victory threw the club into terrible disciplinary trouble, and through no fault of our own.

For some reason the Football League allowed the match referee to be wired with a microphone for a Channel Four programme. It was a ridiculous scheme in an attempt to gauge on-field behaviour by professional First Division players. How it was agreed I will never know and someone forgot to tell the Arsenal players anything about it.

The battleground of a First Division football match is a highly charged, emotional arena and there are certain things that go on that should never come to the attention of the public. Not serious offences, just every-match occurrences that are best kept in-house. Back-chat with referees, players talking to each other, moans and groans, swearing. I can't believe that any other sport would allow an intrusion into private lives like the League allowed on Saturday, 11 February.

Our skipper, Tony Adams, was seen and heard calling Harrow referee David Elleray names when a clear goal was disallowed. David Rocastle also got involved. When the programme came out the Channel Four anchorman was Tommy Docherty and he took great delight in criticising Arsenal. The Doc gave the programme a platform and just

On the bus touring North London and it's smiles on wheels.

hammered nails into us. It must be nice for Tommy to have led such a whiter than white existence and conducted his life without any controversy!

It was a programme that didn't do the game any good. Channel Four had said that the film would be shown in front of League and PFA representatives before it went out but that never happened and Arsenal took the brunt of fierce criticism and huge headlines the following day. There were calls for the club and Tony Adams to be charged with bringing the game into disrepute and I am just grateful that football saw sense in the end. Had the programme been shown today I am convinced that the club would have been in real trouble because attitudes have definitely hardened inside Lancaster Gate. If Norwich skipper Ian Butterworth can be charged for making comments on his own club call line then anything goes as far as I am concerned. It is sad, but a fact of football that the game needs to look at itself.

The public just can't relate to situations like the "bugged" Millwall game, especially armchair viewers. The boss was seen going into the referee's room to give David Elleray a right rollicking only to freeze when he saw the camera. But a manager surely is entitled to express his point of view to a referee. A good goal had been disallowed and at the end of the day it is our livelihood which is at stake. Tony Adams, for instance, was never given a chance to explain his on-field actions on camera. They just used a clip of his demonstration and left the public to make up their own minds, with Docherty firing the bullets.

It was, however, a great victory at newly promoted Millwall, a team who had led the First Division at one stage. But now we were top and determined to stay there, despite Liverpool going like a train behind us and the pressure, hyped by the media, building up. There is talk of the title, of course, but it is played down inside Highbury.

We lost at home to Forest, a disastrous result, and then completed two dreadful performances in front of our fans by drawing 2-2 with Charlton. That is just one point out of six, hardly Championship form, and we knew we had to win at Southampton on 25 March. We did, 3-1, and the boss described it as one of our best displays of the season.

Then George Graham produced a change of tactic that probably won the title for Arsenal. At Manchester United on 2 April, and in a live TV game, he introduced the sweeper system with just eight matches to go. It was a brave, bold decision and one that would either work or blow up in his face.

The players were not told until the Friday morning when the boss explained that David O'Leary would sweep behind Steve Bould and Tony Adams with full-backs Lee Dixon and Nigel Winterburn pushing up. Michael Thomas, Kevin Richardson and David Rocastle would play in midfield with Alan Smith up front and me supporting down the left. George felt we had been getting bogged down and had to try and bring sides on to us. At Highbury especially we were struggling to break sides down. So it was now or

North London goes wild with delight as Arsenal bring the trophy home. I just about find room to wave to the crowd.

never for Arsenal and George Graham and not even he could have believed how well we would adapt.

We practised the system just once, on that Friday, and it went surprisingly well. I enjoyed the free role the sweeper system gave me. The lads took to it quickly and we should have won at United. Tony put us ahead with a brave diving header and then had the misfortune to divert in an own goal in the last minutes.

The own goal triggered off more embarrassing scenes for Tony, who had been living through ridiculous "donkey" taunts for the whole of the season. The United fans started up and the newspapers went to town on Monday morning. The *Daily Mirror* even had a picture of him wearing donkey ears and we all thought that was the lowest form of journalism. In fact the club took the paper to the PFA.

I don't know who started the cruel donkey jibes but I only have admiration for Adams about the way he handled the situation. He lived through carrots being thrown on the pitch, inflatable carrots bobbing around the terraces and the continuous taunts of visiting supporters. A lot of players would have gone under but Tony stood firm, showed his character and emerged from the season a better person and, I believe, a better player.

He also ended the season with the perfect answer, the Championship trophy in his hand and held aloft at Anfield in front of millions of TV viewers.

In a funny way the donkey experience probably helped him and drove him on. I have always felt that he needs to be wound up and what he lived through kept him at the very peak of determination. Adams is vital to Arsenal, scores goals from set-pieces and puts his head in where it hurts. When Tony eventually retires and counts up his medals and looks at the things he won during his career I'm sure he will look back on season 1988-89 as the winter he really grew up.

We were still top and looking over our shoulders at Liverpool. At one stage of the season they were so far behind us but now the race was on and it was heading for a great climax.

Arsenal beat Everton at home with goals from Lee Dixon and big Niall Quinn and then we beat Newcastle at Highbury, a game which proved to be my last appearance of the season. I had been feeling twinges in my achilles heel for some time. It wasn't a bad injury but enough to nag away at the back of my mind and restrict me slightly when I ran. I had been to see various people about it, had a series of injections and was then finally told by a specialist, Basil Helal, that I needed an operation. I hoped that the operation would be delayed until after the season because I was desperate to play in the run-in but he advised me to go straight in, get the achilles seen to and not run the risk of further damage.

It was the only option open to me and came as a result of all the road running I did at Sheffield under Wilkinson. There had always been a doubt at the back of my mind, especially after Dr Sash had almost blocked my transfer to Arsenal because of the problem. It was, however, a relief to know exactly what the problem was. There is no question that it had been affecting my running. I would have done anything to stay in the side and yet I was struggling and it was pleasing to score the only goal of the game against Newcastle.

The pressure was on but there were no signs of strain from the boss as we fought to stay ahead of Liverpool. They were winning matches and so were we and the manager didn't get close to us as he nursed Arsenal through the most critical weeks of the season. He is very much the boss and that is the way it should be; any clowning and joking in the dressing-room is left to Theo. They are a good double act.

As with Howard Wilkinson, the players either like or respect George and most of us respected him at that time. He had to make difficult and tough decisions. Verdicts that were going to upset professionals but that was his job as far as we were concerned then.

May Day brought a fantastic performance over Norwich, live on television, and we hit peak form in a 5-0 victory. It was so frustrating to watch and yet I was delighted for the lads. The newspapers were full of the million dollar question – would it be Arsenal or could Liverpool catch them?

Suddenly and sadly, football was rocked by the Hillsborough disaster when 95 Liverpool fans died at the semi-final in Sheffield. It was a tragedy that no one could believe and Liverpool, understandably, postponed all matches in Cup and League while supporters were buried and memorial services held. The club and Merseyside were allowed to mourn in private.

It was a strange situation for football generally and one that meant we had to keep on winning and then wait for Liverpool to play all their matches at the end of the season. One decision was made – our League game at Anfield was put back until Friday 26 May, the last day of the season, and likely to be the Championship decider.

We beat Middlesbrough away with a Martin Hayes goal but then suffered a major blow – Arsenal lost at home to Derby. I had my operation the following Monday and it was a bitterly disappointing weekend. There were two games to go now and we simply had to beat Wimbledon at Highbury the following Wednesday. I couldn't believe it when, listening to the radio at home with my heel up on a cushion, we only managed a 2-2 draw.

The critics were saying we had blown it. I was not so sure and no one at the club was conceding defeat. The agony was that we had to wait nine days before the Liverpool match and until they finished we would not know what we had to do to break the Merseyside Championship monopoly. It was a knife-edge finish to the season.

Friday 26 May, Anfield. Arsenal had to win 2-0 at Liverpool to lift the title for the first time since 1971. It was mission impossible, or was it?

I love to be involved and was determined to travel with the lads to Liverpool. My heel was stitched but nothing was going to stop me getting on that bus when it pulled away from London Colney on our journey into the unknown. No one was quite sure what was going to happen and you could cut the atmosphere with a knife. I always try to be bright and cheerful around Highbury and I believe that the manager likes the social banter in the dressing-room.

There was no special build-up to the biggest game in the lives of most of the players. A few of the squad played cards and then the boss dealt his first ace of the day. He plugged in a video of the year Arsenal won the League and Cup double and told all the lads to watch it. George didn't stop the film or talk through it, he just let us see how the season built up, saw us experience the goals and excitement and watched the climax of that season almost 20 years ago when Arsenal won at Tottenham and Wembley in the same week to do the double. There was plenty of mickey-taking, especially about the gaffer's long sideboards, but all the lads knew that the manager had put the video on for a purpose. "I just wanted them to realise what it was like to win something big," he admitted afterwards.

George Graham didn't put a foot wrong all day. After the lads had lunch at a hotel close to Liverpool and then rested and slept in their beds, we were all called together for a team meeting before boarding the coach again to go to Anfield. The boss told them: "Listen, we are not expected to do this. No-one believes that Liverpool are going to lose at home 2-0.

George Graham, the 1988-89 Manager of the Year with his trophies.

Don't worry about that, it's been a great season and you are a credit to this great club. And you never know, at half-time it could be 0-0, then we might score a goal around 75 minutes and nick victory in the last minutes. Don't forget, if we score they will be looking over their shoulder."

Not even George Graham, I'm sure, could have guessed that his predictions would be spot on.

The dressing-room was relaxed, the lads were buoyant and happy about playing. We'd had a rest from competition and the mood was good. It would probably have been different had we been in Liverpool's shoes, at home and defending a result. That would have created far more anxiety.

I was determined to sit in the dugout and went down the tunnel before the others to take my place. This was the biggest moment of my career and there was no way I was going to sit in the crowd along with the Liverpool supporters. I felt sorry for Niall Quinn and Paul Davis, who had to mix with the home fans in the stand. I understood that the boss wanted his staff on the touchline but I believe it meant more to someone like Davis, who had been through so much after his unfortunate incident with Southampton and the subsequent ban.

Tony Adams was an inspiration all the way through and set the tone in the first minute with a clattering tackle on John Aldridge. From that moment the sleeves were rolled up and determination pumped through every Arsenal vein. No one played with fear, the game started to go to plan and there was a good atmosphere on the bench. George sat upstairs in the first half and it was left to Theo and Pat Rice, the skipper of the double side and now youth team manager, to make the most noise. The players can't hear and yet it helps release the tension. It is not long before I am shouting and screaming instructions just like everyone else.

Half-time and 0-0. George likes everyone to sit down in the dressing-room at half-time while he talks and gives orders. Physio Gary Lewin attended to knocks and bruises and there was a calmness about the Arsenal team. Everyone got up together and moved towards the door. The message was simple, just 45 minutes away from the greatest prize of all.

A goal! Smith scores after 52 minutes with a glancing header. Hand ball? Offside? Liverpool are complaining and Kenny Dalglish is ranting and raving at the officials. It seems an age before referee David Hutchinson gives the verdict to Arsenal.

How long to go? Stewart Houston, the reserve team manager, is keeping the watch and he must get fed up with the same question every few minutes: "How long?" "How long?" The whistles from the Liverpool fans were screaming from every corner of Anfield. It was time. "How long, Stewart?" Nearly into injury time and now John Barnes has it close to our corner flag.

I can't believe it. Barnes tries to dribble and Kevin Richardson nicks the ball and slips it to John Lukic in goal. John throws it to Lee,"How long?", and our full-back pushes it further upfield to Alan Smith. "How long?" Stewart is not looking at his watch now and Smith sends Michael Thomas chasing through the middle. He's through, he's going to score . . . GOAL!

The final whistle. The Championship. Total chaos.

I limped around hugging and kissing everyone and the Anfield stewards pleaded with the Arsenal players not to go too near our fans. They clearly had Hillsborough on their minds. Niall and Paul were now on the pitch, the directors' box had been switched to the middle of Anfield, few fans were running around, it was a lovely place to be.

From nowhere someone produced the Championship trophy and then it was in Tony's hands, held aloft. Then we all got our hands on the biggest prize of all and no one wanted to get off that pitch. Arsenal just wanted to savour the greatest finish in the history of the Championship. The last day of the season, the last kick . . . absolutely incredible.

The dressing-room was like Christmas Day. It was party time with champagne and people popping in to say well done. The first person I bumped into was Gordon Taylor and then a few of the Liverpool lads popped their heads around the door. Peter Beardsley was gracious in defeat,

Bruce Grobbelaar shook his fist playfully at Michael Thomas and Ronnie Moran and Roy Evans both said well done. There was a word of warning, however, from Moran who, before he left us to our private party, said: "Congratulations, you bastards, but don't forget, everyone will want to knock you off your perch next season."

It was reality through the haze of happiness. And you couldn't but admire Liverpool. After all they had been through with Hillsborough they came so close to doing the double themselves and I realised as the champagne corks exploded just how much pressure the club have lived with over the years to stay at the top.

The Arsenal players and staff sang all the way home. Our destination was a club at Enfield and I quickly rang Lesley to tell her that I wouldn't be home. She was having her own celebration with some neighbours and it seemed that the whole of North London was partying when we arrived in our own backyard.

Arsenal drank themselves sober that night. The boss and Theo weren't at the club, it was the players' turn to relish something that you strive for all your career. I had asked the boss on the way back what meant the most to him, winning the League as a player or manager and he didn't even have to think about the reply. "As a manager," he said. "Because when you are in charge you have to concern yourself with everyone's problems."

I felt sorry for Lee Dixon because he had arranged to stay north and return to his family home in the Manchester area. I'm sure he would have preferred to have been with us. It was a happy bunch of Arsenal footballers who left the club in daylight and headed off home to savour the result over mugs of hot coffee.

My Championship medal took pride of place in my home for a few days but is now safely locked up in a bank vault for my children to enjoy in the future.

Football may never experience a finish like it again and what a fantastic achievement for George Graham in only his third season as Arsenal manager. Graham has already proved himself one of the top men in the game. If I have one criticism of him, however, it is that he doesn't praise the players enough. He was oozing pride on the return journey but didn't give himself to the players who, with him, had done it over nine long months. I am sure he appreciates his squad and yet he doesn't come into the dressing-room enough and say, "Fantastic lads, well done."

Perhaps he finds it difficult to express himself. Howard Wilkinson once said to me: "I have got a great bunch of lads, but I never tell them." That is wrong but there is a lot of George Graham in Howard when it comes to expression. Inwardly, he knows we are good. From a skill point of view we are not the best team in the land but for character and spirit there is no stopping us. The Arsenal spirit during the season was special and it is what got us through. The mix of people was right and I'm sure the boss goes into players' characters and backgrounds before he signs them. Everyone looks after each other and the boss would have created that more by design than accident.

A lot of the Arsenal players think that George is strict and fierce but he is nothing compared to Howard Wilkinson. George gives rollickings and then tries to explain himself when the dust has settled. That is not necessary because if a player deserves a rollicking he should get one.

There is no question that the Arsenal manager has a cold front and I wouldn't be surprised if someone, at some time in his career, has hurt him and forced the blinds up. It may have made him determined not to let that situation develop again. The "front" he portrays, however, is not the real man. Underneath there is a jovial person who likes a good time. But he only trusts a few people and you don't get close to George Graham.

But if that is the way he believes he can get success then who am I or anyone else for that matter to argue against him? He won the League for Arsenal, something that a lot of outstanding managers had tried to do for almost 20 years.

I just hope that, like Howard, George doesn't create a monster of himself. If things went wrong he would probably get more stick, simply because of the way he treats people and refuses to open up. When the chips are down that might turn against him.

People who know George Graham well can't believe how he sometimes treats his players. At the end of the 1988-89 season, however, he could do no wrong. As far as North London was concerned, George Graham was king of the castle, the Manager of the Year and everyone's friend.

Chapter Seven
THE MONEY GAME

THE ARSENAL players collected about £15,000 a man for winning the Championship. It was not a one-off reward for that famous victory at Anfield but a collection of win bonuses throughout the season, culminating in the 1988-89 First Division title. Whether you believe that is a lot of money for the ultimate prize in football will have to remain one of the talking points of soccer. The Arsenal players certainly had no idea what kind of bonus the Liverpool stars were on for doing the double!

I was not disappointed with the money side of Arsenal's fantastic achievement because, as I have said before, cash has never been my motivation. And how can you put a price on being Champions? It is every footballer's ambition and outside Merseyside there are not many of us who have got our hands on the trophy over the last ten years. There is also a £300 medal sitting in a bank which means more to me than a £15,000 cheque. I wouldn't sell that medal for £100,000!

The Championship is the professionals' prize. The FA Cup is the glamour while the League is the bread and butter, nine

Coventry goalkeeper Steve Ogrizovic has got the ball but I have got him around the throat!

months' slog which takes in so many obstacles like different playing conditions, pitches, some like concrete, others thick mud, frost, snow, water; then there are injuries to key players to overcome, loss of form and the different styles of the opposition. When you win it and look back there is a great sense of achievement. You feel proud for the club and, yes, proud of yourself.

There were, however, little things about Arsenal's attitude in the Championship season that disappointed the players. The club is so big and powerful that they often give the impression that just playing for one of the best clubs in Britain is enough reward for the staff.

Arsenal, for instance, are the first club I have played for who don't organise a Christmas party for the players' wives and children. Even after we won the title there was no official reception. It was left to the players to rally together and have a celebration party in Covent Garden.

Nor are there players' company cars at Highbury, a perk

I was used to with Sheffield Wednesday. There was a story going around earlier in the Championship season that car giants Rover wanted to present 15 cars to the playing staff but the offer was turned down by the club because there was not enough money involved. We have no idea whether that story is true but it only added to the nag that Arsenal could do more for the people they employ.

It was Alan Ball who once said that you are made aware of wearing the Arsenal shirt. I know exactly what he means although I don't completely believe that Arsenal are aware of what the players did for the club.

The question of contracts and bonuses also brought a few raised eyebrows in the dressing-room after we had won the title. I knew that I had signed for the same basic wage that I was on at Sheffield Wednesday and was happy to be financially rewarded under the incentive scheme that exists at Highbury. The higher you are in the first Division and the more trophies you win, the greater the reward. It is similar to other clubs, and the right way to go about things.

What I didn't realise was that Arsenal's bonus scheme hadn't been changed or improved for ten years. When I found that out I couldn't believe that a club like Arsenal had been allowed to stick with a ten-year-old scheme. Good for them, as they got away with it, and whoever negotiated the deal a decade ago should become prime minister!

Questions, however, were asked and Tony Adams, as skipper, and I, because I had taken over from Paul Davis as the PFA representative, had meetings with George Graham. To his credit, the boss was always on the players' side and during the summer of 1989 a new bonus scheme was written and some players were given new contracts in order to reward them for their efforts.

I think the club made another mistake, though, in not giving all players new deals. Lee Dixon, Steve Bould, Nigel Winterburn and Tony Adams collected but others didn't. Kevin Richardson asked and was turned down and I was certainly never approached. I just believe that it would have been the ultimate thank you and it wasn't as if the club couldn't afford it!

The scoreboard says Arsenal 0 Coventry 0, but not for long as I score the first goal.

Bonuses at all clubs are linked to winning cups and Arsenal's, of course, are more realistic because, as one of the top five in the country, they have a real chance of cashing in. At Sheffield Wednesday we were on incredible money to go top of the First Division but, realistically, the club knew it would never happen. We were a fifth-to-12th position club and Wednesday set their bonuses accordingly.

At Hull we once got £50 for every goal we scored which sounds like a good incentive but does backfire on the club. We once lost 7-3 at Brentford and the sting of that defeat was smoothed by £150 extra on pay day!

Arsenal's bonus scheme now is top class and that is the way it should be. I know they like to be tight on the purse strings and have bills to pay and yet the present first-team squad has generated thousands and thousands of pounds for the club and should be rewarded properly. Winning the Championship also opens up many doors for the club. Sponsorship deals are offered, clubs from all over the world want to play you and competitions are especially organised just so the Champions of England can be invited. And the name of Arsenal Football Club is big box office.

One such competition was sponsored by Zenith Data Systems and a trip to Miami to play Independiente at the start of the 1989-90 season caused a lot of friction amongst the players. The managing director of Zenith spoke to one of our players and told him that the club was earning a lot of money from the trip. There was nothing underhand in the conversation, they were just chatting about football and Arsenal's new season. What he didn't realise, however, was that the players' reward for the five-day trip was just £500. That may sound a lot of money to the man in the street but not when you realise just how much cash the club are generating as Champions, or from the deal they signed with Zenith.

It triggered more discussions between the manager and us and, coming at the same time as a new bonus scheme was being thrashed out, it got a little out of hand. There was a time when the players thought they were being "sold down the river".

Fortunately everything was resolved. We didn't get any further reward for that Miami trip, but promises were made for future events and the new bonus deal on contracts was agreed. And once again George Graham was true to his word. In the meetings that I and Tony Adams had with him he agreed with us that the players should be rewarded properly and he said that he would report that fact to the board. He was our go-between and we had to believe him and, to be fair to him, he did sort it out.

It was strange for me to be discussing contracts and money with the manager after just one full season at Highbury. But I had been elected by the players to be their Union representative and it is something I take very seriously. I only go into jobs like this wholeheartedly and whatever I do I hope the eventual aim is for the good of the game.

Another dressing-room decision at Highbury was to organise a players' pool for the entire 1989-90 season, a pool that would generate a cash flow for the staff to share. It was not something we decided to do on the spur of the moment and we wanted it

Happiness is a goal . . .

. . . and I'm proud of my career scoring record.

to be well run and dovetailed by someone outside the club. A number of agents were discussed and we came down eventually to Jerome Anderson, a man who runs his own financial and marketing business and who is a friend of many of the first-team squad.

Jerome and I started to organise a number of events and we turned our attention to functions like golf days, a book about the Champions, a video, a celebration dinner and a clothing deal with a company called Farah. There was also charity work just to prove that it was not all take by the Arsenal players. We were all in it together and everything was done with the club's permission. Arsenal had to give it the OK because any bad publicity would reflect badly on them. We didn't feel that we were doing anything differently from the manager who had his own agent to endorse a number of products, and who was getting paid accordingly. George Graham, as manager of the Champions, was big business and the players had no complaints. They just decided to take advantage of being top of the tree for once. The manager spoke to us about the pool and told us to make sure that it was done properly. He wanted us to do well out of it but insisted we kept our credibility and he was always in the background, keeping a watchful eye on proceedings.

There were 22 people in the pool, including physio Gary Lewin, kit man Tony Donelley and fringe squad players Kevin Campbell, Alan Miller and Stephen Morrow. We discussed the boss coming in but he was doing very well on his own and good luck to him. We certainly didn't worry about what George was earning because he was simply maximising his own potential. Players can become jealous, especially where money is concerned and yet a manager's job is hard enough, a 24-hours-a-day existence and if promotions people think he is worth marketing, that is up to them. The one thing the manager's outside activities did do, however, was make it difficult for him to say no to us. But he did go through the roof after a Championship dinner organised by us resulted in front-page publicity and controversy for Arsenal.

We organised a Championship stag night dinner with guests paying for their tickets and for the privilege of having an Arsenal player on their table. Norman Collier was the comedian and the son of the managing director of Farah was one of the guests we had invited. The problems began when Collier was telling his jokes. He didn't go down very well and a few people slipped off to the bar, including Arsenal players Paul Merson and Steve Bould. There was a bit of shouting and heckling although none, I'm certain, from Merson and Bould.

At the end of the evening everyone went into the bar and Paul did get upset when the chairman of the supporters club, Barry Baker, approached him and asked him for a home telephone number. Paul didn't believe it was the right time or place, an argument resulted, others joined in and there was some pushing and shoving. It certainly wasn't as bad as the papers eventually made out and Paul and Steve were not involved in the alleged beating up of one fan. I have also heard reports that Merson was screaming and shouting from the bar and was then sick everywhere but that is simply not true. They simply paid the penalty for being the Arsenal players involved in the pushing and shoving and it was their names which became plastered over the newspapers.

The headlines were the last thing that Merson needed, especially after an incident a few weeks earlier when it was claimed he had a fight using a snooker cue. This time, at least, he had witnesses and he and Steve had certainly gone home before the police arrived. I had also left by the time the so-called punch up happened and knew nothing about it until eleven the next morning when Jerome contacted me and said: "We have got problems, the press are involved."

Paul Merson and I have become quite close since I signed for Arsenal. I pick him up most mornings and take him to the training ground at London Colney and have spoken to him, and listened, for many hours. I spoke to him and Steve about the dinner and they insisted that they had nothing to do with the fighting, although they apologised for being loud. They'd had an argument but had certainly not got involved with anything physical.

In my naïvety I was prepared to leave it at that. The press news boys had already got hold of the boss, however, and this was the first Arsenal had heard about any problems. George Graham contacted Jerome for an explanation and the next morning the front pages were full of Arsenal and bad-boy Merson. This time it was my turn to ring Jerome. "You're right," I said. "We have got problems."

There were repercussions immediately. Rumblings from inside Highbury suggested that the players' pool should be dropped and Farah were having second thoughts about their clothing contract with us. The press were still hammering the story and it couldn't have been worse. Steve and Paul volunteered to come out of the player pool but the boss wanted action in some way. He decided that Bould would be fined for his part in the bad publicity and Paul Merson was suspended by the club. It was a disastrous ending to an event that I had helped organise and a terrible blow for Paul, whom I like and have been trying to help.

I have got a lot of time for Paul Merson and in some ways treat him like a brother. He is misunderstood by a lot of people although he has to accept that he can only be helped so much and the rest has got to come from him. He has had one or two problems and he tells me that he does find the off-field pressures of being a household name and a professional with one of the biggest clubs in Britain hard to handle. The fact is that he is only doing what every other 21-year-old guy is doing in the country – only if he makes one mistake he gets slaughtered for it.

That, though, is the lesson. When you are playing for Arsenal and are high profile you can't afford to step out of line. He will find that every mistake he makes for the next few years will be monitored, especially by people who don't know him but like to knock "names" off their perch. I'm sure there are those critics who think that he is a complete nutter and it is how Paul deals with that pressure which is going to hold the key to his future.

There is a side to Merson that people don't see. He is a sincere, honest bloke and if we can all help him recognise his responsibilities as a public figure he will be a huge success. It may take months, years, but I know he can become one of the outstanding talents in English football.

109

Paul should take encouragement from Tony Adams. They are both around the same age and look how Tony has made himself cope with the pressure of the country-wide donkey taunts. He has emerged as a better player and a stronger character.

There is no questioning Merson's talent. If he gets everything else together he could easily go all the way and I can certainly see him leading the line for England. It is only his reputation holding him back at the moment because on ability alone, there is no problem. He is 21 now and if he can get to 34 without injury or mishap there should be no reason why he need work again. His talent would make enough money to retire. There are not many players who can say that and I can see him being as big box office as Bryan Robson and Kevin Keegan.

All he has to do is make sacrifices. He should realise that he is hurting his nearest and dearest when he does go off the rails. I feel sick to the teeth when he gets in trouble, and I am not family. Paul is the first player I have come across who has threatened to throw his career away and he has certainly reached the crossroads. He can only go one of two ways and I just hope that he makes the right turning. It's got to be worth it.

George Graham had no option but to come down hard on Paul and Steve. The club had to be seen to take action. I felt sorry for Steve because he had been going through a rotten time with injuries. But the boss said that any bad behaviour in public was not acceptable and, of course, he was right.

It was also decided by the players that Bould and Merson should be pulled out of the clothing contract just to prove to Farah that, as a group of men, we were proud of Arsenal's image.

It was a bitterly disappointing start to Arsenal's title defence and one that brought a lot of bad publicity down on the club. It was the last thing that Jerome Anderson, I and the players' committee wanted and, indeed, expected. A club like Arsenal should be seen to be leading the field in everything that it does. It simply has to be whiter than white with a stain-free image.

Chapter Eight
THE PLAYERS' UNION

THE PROFESSIONAL Footballers' Association was formed 83 years ago to carry out one purpose, to look after the interests of all the players in this country. Before I joined the management committee in December 1988 I didn't realise how big and powerful it is. The union is currently going from strength to strength.

I had been a delegate at Hull and first got involved in a serious way when, staying at the Noke Hotel, St Albans, where I signed for Arsenal from Sheffield Wednesday, I had a chance meeting with Brian Talbot, now manager of West Bromwich Albion but then chairman of the PFA. We discussed many aspects of football that night and he said that I would do a good job on the union's management committee. I have always been interested in the running of the game and keen to be involved with things other than just playing, and so I was interested in Talbot's plan.

My union life developed from there. I applied for election, Arsenal team-mate Alan Smith proposed me, and I was elected on to a committee which today consists of Garth Crooks

Who's that with Brian Marwood?

(Charlton), the chairman, Gordon Taylor, chief executive, Brendon Batson, deputy chief executive, Gary Mabbutt (Spurs), Trevor Morgan (Colchester), Clive Baker (Barnsley), Colin Gibson (Manchester United), Lawrie Sanchez (Wimbledon), George Berry (Stoke) and myself.

I have been so impressed with the PFA since my involvement, and have watched its growth so enthusiastically, that I don't see how in the future it can't become one of the controlling bodies of the game along with the Football League and Football Association. It is a big organisation and I don't see the point in three different bodies all pulling their own way, instead of the three fighting together for the good of the game. Our secret is that we have the confidence and respect of the players, the people who, along with the fans, make football what it is in the country today. Without players and spectators there would be no soccer and a lot of people should remember that.

Each player in the country pays £25 a year to join the union and for that outlay they can call on us to help them in any way, privately and professionally. The union helps players with contracts, pensions, business, education, contract disputes, injuries, fitness, compensation, anything that is linked to the game. It is not a bad return for £25 a year, is it? We are simply pushing for a better career and future for our members.

A short time ago a player got a percentage of any transfer fee but that levy has now gone to the PFA and the money is invested for the individual. Instead he receives a lump sum when he retires. Everything is geared to benefiting the player and when he moves he can still negotiate his own signing-on fee which is legally written into his contract.

The man at the centre of the union is Gordon Taylor. It is probably clear by now that I like people who have a burning love for the game and a desire for the future to be even brighter. Taylor fits perfectly into that category. I know it is easy for me to say but the sooner Taylor is the top man in soccer, the overall supremo, the better the sport will be. He has total respect from the players and they made it clear how much he meant to them when in June 1989 the League and new President Bill Fox wanted Gordon as their chief executive. But Fox didn't get total backing from his management committee and they didn't welcome him with open arms. It cost them a good man and I believe the way the League mucked him about made Gordon realise what a good position he was in with us. Taylor, I'm certain, saw the turmoil the League was in and realised that he wouldn't get the backing of everyone at their headquarters.

My greatest fans, daughters Charlotte (left) and Sophie.

I still can't believe they let him go and it was certainly to our benefit. There is no such turmoil at the PFA and the players are right behind their leader.

The PFA committee discussed the Taylor case for many hours. Had we thought that Taylor going would have benefited the future of the game we probably wouldn't have fought so hard to keep him. But we soon realised that the League didn't deserve him and that Taylor could make more impact on the future with the players.

I like to think that all the men sitting on the PFA management committee have the sport at heart. There are no egos, we are not out to gain anything for ourselves. We are just a group of professionals trying to fight for the future of the players. We meet every eight weeks in Manchester and the meetings usually last from ten in the morning until six at night. There is a lot to discuss and report and then, of course, there is the daily work done by Gordon and his full-time employees.

The hardest situation we are trying to cope with is the current climate of censorship on and off the pitch. It covers a wide range of problems, from players talking to referees, players' behaviour and how it is controlled and the punishment handed out by the FA and League. My fear is that we are not keeping a balance and players have become too worried even to talk about the game. The fear of suspension and fine is now so great that the FA are in danger of taking away the wonderful expression, passion and feeling that is the hallmark of the game.

No, I'm not saying players should be allowed to argue or even scrap on the pitch but it has to be treated carefully. We are so quick these days to take a minor situation and blow it up into a riot. I remember Kevin Keegan and Billy Bremner throwing their shirts down at Wembley after a Charity Shield dust up. What would have happened to those two world-names today? I wonder if they would have been banned for life!

During the 1989-90 season Arsenal was involved in two ugly incidents. Early in the season a 20-man brawl resulted at the end of our game against Norwich at Highbury and Gordon Taylor asked me to hold a small investigation, despite the fact that I had not been playing and only discovered the facts after I returned home from a reserve match.

There are many details to resolve. Norwich player Malcolm Allen, now at Millwall, was at fault early on with an elbow at David O'Leary and that went unpunished by referee George Tyson. Arsenal were given two dubious penalties and that annoyed the Norwich side. I have to draw the conclusion that the referee could have helped the situation by stamping down early on and being stronger. We were then confused by the fact that Tyson said that he wasn't going to report the brawl and then changed his mind after the massive headlines the game received. I am not excusing any of the players for pushing and shoving each other and it is not good for the game to see professionals running half the length of the field to get involved. But was the referee at fault? Could he have stopped it happening?

Once it hit the headlines the bandwagon began. The referees' society defended their man, the police said the clubs should be relegated, Norwich even disciplined their skipper Ian Butterworth for making comments on the club call telephone line and the pressure mounted on the FA. They had to act, disregarding the guilt, disregarding how they really felt. Norwich were fined £50,000, Arsenal £20,000 but I can't help wondering how this would have been treated 15 years ago and what the outcome would have been then? I just feel that it is the in-thing to treat footballers like criminals these days. I accept that there is more over-reacting and that silly niggly things go on but has it really deteriorated that much? One thing is sure, the media treatment is over the top and that puts pressure on the FA, the police and anyone else who wants to jump on the bandwagon.

These people should realise that they are in danger of killing the game off. If only they would sit back and analyse before always kicking the game in the teeth. It seems to me that some people want a sending-off, a fight or a controversial incident just to generate their own brand of excitement. I find it sad, and very worrying.

I did take stick from inside Highbury after being asked by the PFA to hold a mini-inquiry into the Norwich game. The players joked about me stitching them up and George Graham gave me a ticking-off for getting involved. I had to calm him down and assure him that I was simply passing back information in an effort to establish the truth.

The PFA is always making players aware of their responsibilities, on and off the field, but the argument comes back that they are being punished for nothing. They worry that it is a crime to do the slightest thing. And the punishments are definitely tougher, often for minor offences.

After we had lost at Aston Villa a group of Arsenal players surrounded the linesman at the end of the game to ask about Villa's second goal, scored by Derek Mountfield. There was no sending-off, no pushing, no complaint from the referee but after a few headlines like, "They're at it again", the FA reacted and at one stage it looked as though we might be on a second disrepute charge. I had to explain to the players, as the PFA man, that professionals today can't do that sort of thing. The fact that footballers have been protesting ever since the game was invented doesn't matter, today the rules are different and a lot tougher.

The inconsistency by referees is an old chestnut but one that really worries us. Some officials you can talk to, discuss an incident, complain, swear at and they will continue to control the game superbly. Next week you make the same comment and you are off.

Neil Midgley is as good as they come. The players respect him and yet he was the central figure in an incident that perfectly illustrates what I am talking about. When we beat Stoke in the FA Cup in January 1990 Perry Groves was hauled down in full flow by defender Cliff Carr. Midgley didn't even book him and the lad knew he was lucky because another referee would have sent him off.

What happens then if Tony Adams is the defender who commits a similar rugby tackle on an opposing forward and is shown the red card? We are supposed to live by the same rules and yet it all comes down to the interpretation of one man. Are you telling me that in front of 40,000 people, perhaps live on television, an Arsenal player would not have been punished for that sort of challenge!

I once took a penalty at Norwich and scored, only for the referee to demand it to be taken again because two players had moved into the area. Technically correct, but every week referees allow a penalty to stand even when three or four players run into the box. Again, no logic, no consistency and I am not just complaining because I missed the retake!

Where has the change come from that makes the media over-react, referees alter, the FA get tougher? Was it Heysel? Is it simply the 1990s? It seems football is always blamed as a society problem and yet I look at rugby and see fighting and players stamping on one another. I watch ice hockey with violent punch-ups taking place and wait for the public outcry. But it never comes. A few footballers push and shove each other and all hell breaks loose.

Paul Gascoigne had a push and shove with John Bumstead at Chelsea and Gazza stayed in the papers for a week. I am not saying he was right to flare up, but I do say that there is one rule for football, and another for the rest. When rugby players exchange blows it is not a real problem. When a football star is sent off for fighting it is behaviour to incite a riot.

The PFA is heavily involved with discipline. Managers ring up to ask the union's opinion about a player's behaviour and how he should be punished, or the player complains because he feels he has been hard done by. The PFA's attitude is that if we feel he has been hard done by we will help him fight his case, if we believe he has done wrong the manager will be told to carry out the punishment.

Gordon Taylor was involved in the strange incident when former QPR manager Trevor Francis fined Martin Allen for walking out on the club on match day to be with his wife at the birth of his first child. Gordon and George Graham also spoke about the Villa incident. They agreed a punishment and four players were fined. It enabled Arsenal to explain to the FA that the matter had been dealt with internally and, fortunately, they didn't take it any further.

There is also tremendous fear in the game. Professionalism has taken over and is gripping soccer by the throat. The pressure that men find themselves under to win is ridiculous. There is the manager under pressure to win or be sacked; the chairman who kicks his manager out even though he won promotion the previous season; the chairman who sacks the manager because the manager doesn't smile enough; the player who is frightened to lose his place. If we don't get a 0-0 draw I'll lose my job, is the talk of the Nineties. The game is not more physical but, my God, it is harder to be a professional footballer these days.

Are the characters being driven out by the pressure? There are only a handful now and people like Paul Gascoigne are continually knocked. Sure, he is making a good living but it seems that too many people want to stop him doing what he is good at.

Arsenal, for instance, don't have a so-called character. I don't believe George Graham would sign one – he feels they are too much of a liability on and off the field. He feels "we are all in this together" rather than someone who grabs off-field headlines for the wrong reasons.

One new development with the PFA has been to negotiate contracts for players when they change clubs. We are in an era of the agent and the PFA now offers a similar facility. We have set up an advisory company, owning 50 per cent of it with our partners Brian Hassell and David Carr. The PFA decided to act because we became snowed under with complaints of players being ripped off by certain agents. Gordon was also inundated with calls from players inquiring: "What do I ask for when I sign?" We felt we had to do something and a good example came last season when two players signed for the same club for a similar fee. Player A had an agent and paid him £20,000 for negotiating a deal. Player B, under the PFA's watchful eye, handed over just £800 for getting the same contract. That is the difference, and did the agent do any more for his money? I am certainly not against agents and encourage them in the commercial field but all the PFA do is charge by the hour and it works out as a nominal fee compared to some of the agent stories we are told.

The one thing the PFA fear is that a number of agents are in football for their own means. Do they push the price to the limit, for their own 20 per cent? Do they sell a story to a newspaper simply to line their own bank balance? In some cases, I would have to say yes. Some certainly don't have the good of the game at heart.

I don't have an agent as such. Brian Roach has been a friend and advisor since I joined Arsenal and I would trust him with my life. Jerome Anderson is a friend of Arsenal and goes about his business in an honest and professional way. But the good ones are hard to find and players would be better off with the PFA than with an agent who simply wants to line his own pocket.

I love my work with the PFA. It is time-consuming and there is no cash reward and I do it simply because I love football. I wish I had got involved years ago. Every day I learn something about the game and how it is run. The legal side of the game, money owed and the compensation on injuries takes up much of the PFA's time.

There have been many drawn-out, sad cases of players losing their careers through injury. The Danny Thomas situation is one. His professional life was ruined after a tackle. Another boy, a superb athlete, was reduced to a pitiful sight after an incident in training. He is 20 years old and is suing the football club, but how do you put a price on a lifetime in the game, or gear the asking figure to the money that player could have earned over the next 12 years? These are just some of the problems that the PFA deals with and Gordon Taylor is at the centre of the organisation. I am just learning the trade and I put the hours in because I desperately want football to have a great future.

There are so many people with football in their blood, men who work overtime to keep soccer the greatest game in the world. And there is a minority who are in it just to get out of it what they can. They have no love for the sport and the sooner they are dismissed the better.

We are going through a one-hundred-mile-an-hour era with football suffering at the hands of the sensational Nineties. But if we are careful there is no way the game can be beaten. Common sense must prevail.

Chapter Nine

THE TITLE DEFENCE

GEORGE GRAHAM is not a man for looking back. The title had been won, great, but he was already forward planning when we had our first get-together of the new season. The Arsenal manager wanted his club to go on to even greater things and he made it clear that the Championship was just the start of his long-term battle plan for the Gunners. Graham stressed that Arsenal could win the Championship again and he also made it clear that he wasn't happy with our performance in the two major cup competitions, the FA Cup and Littlewoods. He wanted a good run in both and it was obvious that he was planning for years of domination at Highbury, just like Liverpool, the club he admires most of all.

I was slightly surprised that there were no new faces in the squad although the Arsenal manager had always stressed that he would only buy when the right player became available and had no intention of throwing Arsenal's money around.

The summer of 1989 had been non-stop work for me and I had trained alone for weeks building up my fitness and the muscles around my repaired achilles tendon. We had a short family break on Minorca and even then it was up and down the beaches in the sand, pushing myself back to top condition for what I expected to be a great season.

Arsenal expected everyone to be at their best to want to beat the new Champions and we had to be prepared to take on all-comers again. It was going to be tough but, just as Liverpool had proved for so long, we had to make sure that Arsenal were not just a one-season wonder.

I can't thank Arsenal physio Gary Lewin enough for the help and encouragement he gave me in those lonely summer weeks when I arrived for fitness training. He was there by my side all the way through, pushing me on and making sure I did all the running and step-ups that were needed to build up the muscles in the calf and ankle.

It was then into a hectic pre-season with the rest of the players, the first four days at Trent Park, then to London Colney, to Sweden for a series of matches and back to Wembley for the pre-season tournament we won so convincingly the previous year. There was also a trip to Miami for the exhibition money-raising match that caused so many problems over bonuses. We didn't have a chance to stop and think as the new kick-off approached.

In Sweden I soon realised that my general fitness was not yet up to scratch. There was no reaction to my operation but I needed a lot more work before being ready for First Division action. The boss told me to stay behind when the team went to Miami and I didn't play in the pre-season tournament at Wembley and had to be content with slogging away with the reserves. I was bitterly disappointed not to travel to America but the boss was right and deep down I knew that he had to leave me behind to carry on working. I played against Bishops Stortford and Aylesbury and worked with reserve coach Stewart Houston while the lads sunned themselves in Miami and won at Wembley again. Our next hurdle was the Charity Shield at Wembley, the season curtain raiser against Liverpool, and a lot of people were expecting another dish of excitement. Alas, we were not up to it this time and from the subs bench I realised that we had done too much travelling for our own good. It seemed that our legs were in Sweden, our bodies in Florida and our heads at Wembley; we

The defence of the title starts at Old Trafford and Michael Knighton, the man who wanted to be chairman, takes centre stage.

were all over the place and Liverpool's 1-0 victory could have been so much more.

The club obviously made a lot of money out of all the pre-season tournaments and matches and there is no question that when you are Champions the demands on you are greater. Yet it was clear that we had not coped with the pressure and failed to pass the opening examination of being the English League Champions.

The boss selected me for the opening First Division game, away at Manchester United, but I still feared about our preparation. I believe that the players had done too much travelling and once again were all at sea as United stuffed us 4-1. We were not helped by a series of bogus phone calls in the middle of the night that woke up a lot of the players, or a stomach illness to skipper Tony Adams which allowed him to complete only the first 20 minutes. By that time we were 1-0 down.

The United public were in the middle of some amazing hype surrounding proposed new chairman Michael Knighton. He was said to be taking over, had offered millions and millions to chief executive Martin Edwards for control and had already had massive publicity for this big opening game against us. He wasn't going to miss a trick and before the kick-off Knighton raced out on to the pitch with the ball, juggled it, kept it up in the air on his head and clowned around in front of a packed

The title defence starts to go wrong against Norwich at Highbury with a 21-man brawl. George didn't like it when PFA chief executive Gordon Taylor asked me to hold an internal investigation.

house. Not the behaviour of a chairman, you might say, and Knighton, alas, has shown his true colours since. How United fell for it I don't know, yet it certainly set them on fire against Arsenal and although David Rocastle equalised they bombed us in the second half.

We were shell-shocked, drained and half-asleep. The pre-season had finally caught up on us. On the coach returning home after a game a meal is served, then a video played while some players play cards. This time, though, everyone fell asleep within minutes of the coach pulling away from Manchester. Arsenal, one match into the new season as Champions, were simply shattered.

We bounced back against Coventry on the Tuesday night, then drew with Wimbledon at Highbury and thrashed Sheffield Wednesday 5-0. I scored against my old club and that was my 100th League and Cup goal as a professional. It was a good day for me. In fact, I got four goals in the first seven matches and after we had beaten Wednesday so convincingly everyone felt that the bad start was behind us. We had opened up in eighth spot and the ball was rolling again, we were back to normal.

There was one doubt at the back of my mind and that was my relationship with the boss. I hoped that he didn't hold anything against me following our meetings regarding bonuses and players' problems. I only get involved with things to do my best for players and I just hope that he doesn't view me as a threat, a ring leader if you like. I believe you have to stand up and be counted and yet I have seen before what happens to players who have crossed George Graham. Falling out with the manager was the last thing on my mind and the last thing I wanted or needed. I hoped that he looked upon our meetings as simply communications between the players and the manager, and nothing else.

I scored again against Charlton but picked up a niggling little calf strain and missed the away game with Chelsea. This proved to be the start of a series of injuries and set-backs that wrecked my season. The defence of the title had started so well for me and yet for the next few weeks I picked up injuries and couldn't hold down a regular place in the side because of the problems.

The calf strain kept me out for two matches, then I returned against Manchester City at home, only to strain knee ligaments in a collision with Trevor Morley, the striker who was eventually sold to West Ham. Gary Lewin helped me into the dressing-room, diagnosed the problem straight away and went back into the dugout while one of two doctors that Arsenal have on duty on match days, John Crane, examined my knee. It isn't a serious injury but keeps me out for five weeks and that is another terrible blow.

I can only watch the team continue on a route of mixed results that is hardly the form of the best team in the land. We lose at Spurs, lose at Everton and yet knock Liverpool out of the Littlewoods Cup at Highbury with a goal from Alan Smith, who comes off the subs bench to continue our "hold" over our arch rivals.

The team are not playing particularly well and I believe we have been caught up with the fact that we are the Champions and the worry that you have to live up to that title. At times we tried too hard to perform outstandingly well just because the Championship trophy was sitting in the boardroom cabinet.

We had started the season with a flat back four but then the boss reverted to a sweeper system. It was the formation that won Arsenal the title and yet the players are happiest when we are using a 4-4-2 system with Alan Smith and Paul Merson up front and me tucking in on the left side. It will be interesting to see if the sweeper system brings the same results as last season!

Another return from injury, this time at Millwall and the match will be remembered, not for our impressive 2-1 victory, but for the unfortunate incident when David Rocastle swallowed his tongue and had to be revived by Gary Lewin on the pitch. Whenever a player goes down with a head or facial injury I believe that the game should be stopped immediately. There was controversy when referee David Axcell of Southend allowed play to continue for several minutes while Rocky lay unattended. Fortunately Gary got to him in time, freed his tongue and David felt well enough to continue, although clearly dazed.

After the game I was questioned by reporters about the incident, gave my honest views and said that the PFA were concerned about situations when players were struck on the head in a collision. Amazingly, this led to another showdown with the boss.

On the Monday George called me into his office and laid into me for getting involved with an incident that I had nothing to do with. He was furious that I had been quoted in the morning papers about the Rocastle injury, linking it to the PFA. I was staggered and tried to explain to him that I had been approached by reporters and had given some honest answers. Graham, however, told me not to get involved and it is clear to me now that he is worried about my PFA role. This follows my involvement with the infamous game against Norwich when once again the PFA were involved via me. The boss clearly feels I have got too much to say and it is worrying. All I can repeat is that I am only being honest, I am not trying to stir up anything and can't believe that he is worried about my intentions.

The boss keeps me in the side, in a 3-0 victory over Queen's Park Rangers and yet I can't believe it, I am injured again. Then on Monday Jimmy Dyson calls to tell me that my dad, Robert, who has been ill with cancer for a year, is getting weaker and I should travel up to the north-east to see him. I contacted Gary for permission and he called me back after clearing it with the boss. I was grateful to the manager because I only just made it to Seaham in time. My father died 24 hours later.

Watching your father die is a terrible experience and the only good that came out of that traumatic week was the fact that it brought my sister and I back closer together. We had not got on for years for one reason or another and it was always my father's wish that we should make up and be a family again. The emotion and sadness of sitting at his bedside at home healed the wounds between us and at least dad died a happier man.

The next few days were just a blur of tears and emotion. Arsenal had a vital Littlewoods Cup tie at Oldham on Wednesday night but I was so preoccupied with arranging the funeral and looking after mum that I didn't even discover until Thursday morning that we had gone out 3-1. It will not please the boss because I know that he had his heart set on a return to Wembley this season. Perhaps it will come in the FA Cup?

No Cup glory either and former Arsenal skipper, Kenny Sansom, is congratulated by QPR players after scoring the first goal that knocked us out of the FA Cup.

I also made the decision to drop out of the next game, a live TV confrontation with Liverpool at Anfield. Mum wanted me to play but I knew I wasn't in the mood and would not have done justice to myself or the club. We sat at home together in the north-east and watched the repeat of the Anfield Championship decider. It never lived up to that billing, however, and Liverpool were too good for us on the day.

Seven days later and we had another live game, this time at home to United. We needed to take revenge on them for their first-day mauling and I was delighted to return and see Perry Groves score the only goal of the game. The lads were brilliant before the match. I was a bit down and they rallied me and when I watched a video of the game I was pleased to hear George Best say that the difference between the two sides was Marwood. Was he drunk or sober? Only joking, George.

We are top now and yet no one is really satisfied with the way we are playing. Injuries and my father's death have certainly pushed me back and it was great to score in a 3-2 home win over Luton, especially with a header! I hadn't scored since 23 September, amazingly just six games again for me because of my bad luck with injuries. I am proud of my career scoring record however. At the moment it stands at one every three games.

Arsenal, I'm sure, made the mistake of believing all the publicity about them not playing well. I don't believe the manager helped when he kept repeating the fact that we were not the same team as last season. It rubbed off on the players and negative thoughts started to enter our heads. Our attitude, surely, should have been: "We knew it was going to be hard but wait a minute, we are still top of the League." Let's be positive.

It made you realise just how good Liverpool are. Ronnie Moran was right. When the Liverpool coach came into our dressing-room on that great night at Anfield he said that our problems were only just beginning. You have to learn to live with the pressure and we were finding it hard. Yet I believe we made it even harder for ourselves.

Christmas, and I got the worst possible present, another injury at Southampton on Boxing Day. I had collected a slight calf strain against Luton and I soon realised that it was not right and limped for a majority of the game before being substituted. This season is turning into a nightmare and there can't be any more bad luck for me. Injuries, my father's death, there can't be anything else to suffer.

Gary Lewin and I are really getting to know each other. I have been on his treatment table so often we are like blood brothers. This is the fifth injury I have battled through this season and he knows how gutted I am about the whole thing.

This time I miss eight matches. I came back at Charlton with the team desperately needing three points because inconsistent form means we are chasing the title now rather than setting the pace. Selhurst Park, however, is a depressing arena; it's bumpy, windy and an awful 0-0 game. I struggle throughout, not with my injury but with my general play.

My season had been depressing enough without having to endure a couple of incidents over the next few weeks that were to throw a huge question mark over my long-term future at the club. I can't accept either of them and they led to me asking the manager some straight questions.

On 20 January I was sub against Spurs and then totally overlooked the following week. I was then told to train with the reserves only to receive a phone call on Friday afternoon to say that I was in the squad. It was a mystery to me and I contacted Theo to ask him what was going on. He explained that I had been forgotten by the manager.

Forgotten? How do you forget about one of your players at any time, especially before an important FA Cup fourth-round tie against Queen's Park Rangers at Highbury? You are sub v Spurs, then told to train with the reserves, then told you are forgotten and should be in the squad. It didn't make sense and I was not surprised when I didn't make the side in a goalless draw against Rangers.

I wanted to see the boss on Monday to clear things up but at first he refused to see me. He eventually gave me an audience and I said that I could understand not being in the side, but I couldn't accept being forgotten. He said sorry and admitted that the matter hadn't been conducted properly but I could tell that it hurt him to apologise.

We replayed against QPR on Wednesday night. I travelled with the squad but was the odd one out when the side was selected. Arsenal lost 2-0 and that means we are out of both major cup competitions.

Arsenal had a free Saturday and the following Wednesday I played in the reserves at Brighton on a heavy pitch. We won 3-0 and I enjoyed the game despite the fact that it was extremely tiring. I was told to report with the first-team squad on Friday because the boss wanted to work on a particular pattern of play for a game at Hillsborough. I was delighted because I felt my injuries were behind me and with Alan Smith still struggling for goals, my supply to him could be needed.

On Thursday night I felt a slight niggle in my calf and reported it to Gary the following morning. I wasn't concerned about it and pleaded with Lewin not to mention it to the gaffer because I knew that I had a chance of playing. He said he couldn't take that gamble. I knew that I should not have put

Gary on the spot and he was right to mention it to George Graham. The boss came to see me as I was having a bath after training and said that he was disappointed and upset to hear about the injury. "You're upset, what about me after all I have been through?" I said. He walked out after telling me that I would have been substitute.

A few hours later Michael Thomas and Nigel Winterburn went down with injuries and suddenly Arsenal were struggling for players. Gary mentioned to the boss that I was fit to do a job, especially as substitute. The news came back that I was in and back on the coach for Sheffield. That perked me up because the boss obviously had second thoughts and I knew I was fit enough to get through a game. On Saturday he sent me crashing back to square one when he named his side and I was not even substitute. I was devastated, I felt like getting on the first train back home. I felt that George Graham had made me look a mug. I put myself on the line and felt that he had played games with me.

We lost and it was a depressing coach journey back to London. I was sitting at the back feeling low when Gary came to see me and apologised. "You have got nothing to apologise for," I said but Lewin felt that he had set me up. "There is only one person who has set me up," I answered. George Graham had not spoken to me from the moment he sat on the bath the previous day. Lewin tried to explain that the manager felt that it was too much of a gamble to play me.

Enough was enough. What with his complaint to me about talking to the press, our problems with the bonuses and now this, for me it was the final nail in the coffin. The respect that I had built up for him in a year had begun to diminish slightly.

Then came the bombshell. A member of the manager's staff admitted to me that George Graham was trying to teach me a lesson. A lesson! For what? It appears that the boss doesn't like my PFA involvement with the players and this is his way of getting his own back. It is incredible but the truth.

I knew it was impossible to speak to him because a few days earlier he had announced to us that he didn't want any player to see him or talk to him about so-called problems. "I'm the boss, I make the decisions and I won't speak to you" was his attitude.

Was it the pressure of struggling that made George Graham act this way? Arsenal were out of both cup competitions, and we were not looking like Champions. Perhaps it was too much for George to cope with. Yet even when things go well he doesn't treat players particularly well. I returned from Sheffield and said to Lesley: "If ever I become a manager don't let me treat players like that."

I felt that I had done well for George since he signed me. There was even a time when he encouraged me to be in the dressing-room because of my bubbly manner but the relationship was not the same now. It is a tragedy really because my conscience is clear, I have done nothing intentionally to harm my place in the side or upset the boss.

Arsenal bounced back with a fine 3-0 home win over Nottingham Forest. David O'Leary was dropped for this game and it means we have reverted to a flat back four. The players are happy. On Saturday we go to City. Perry is injured and I'm back in and I take great delight in scoring the only goal of the game with a volley and receiving the man of the match award.

I can't believe it. I'm injured again. I like to think I would have stayed in the side but a thigh strain means I have to go back into the treatment room.

A story has appeared in the *Sun* about my problems at Arsenal and, amazingly, it triggers off a meeting with the manager. George calls me in on the morning the story breaks and says that the press are trying to ruin our relationship. He says there is no bad feeling between us and that he only picks teams on ability and performance, nothing else. He tells me that he has never held a grudge against a player and I have nothing to worry about.

I was pleased to talk to the manager but I couldn't believe what he was saying, especially after what I had gone through with him. A member of his staff actually told me that he had been trying to teach me a lesson and now the boss himself says there are no problems. I left the meeting worried about my future at Arsenal. I have a year left and would dearly love to stay and play in the first team again. But if I put my hand on my heart there have to be doubts.

It hasn't escaped me that I am the only player involved in the Championship who hasn't been offered a new contract, or been in a position to turn down fresh terms. To me that is significant but maybe I'm wrong.

I simply can't get over what has happened to me this season. I will still go into the summer with an open mind and wait to see what happens. I have no intention of upsetting George Graham and anything I do or say is done with honesty and clear conscience. I realise that he can make my life a misery and the last thing I want to do is play reserve football for 12 months, especially at my age.

All this has been so upsetting because I have had a great relationship with the club and the last few months have marred a fabulous career for me. My gut feeling is that if I was 100 per cent fit I still wouldn't be first choice, although that won't stop me getting my head down in the summer and trying to prove a few people wrong. I would like to wipe the slate clean and battle back, if I am allowed to. All I can do is wait and see what happens. The ball is very much in George Graham's court.

There are seven games to go and in the closing weeks just three teams left in the title race: us, Liverpool of course, and Villa, who have played magnificently this season under Graham Taylor. Anything can happen although our inconsistency means we can't afford to drop a point. But we do have Villa and Liverpool to play at Highbury. They are live television games and they will surely make or break our season.

Niall Quinn has been sold to Manchester City and all the players at Highbury are delighted for one of the nicest guys around. Niall had to go; his career was stagnating at Arsenal and for a Republic of Ireland International with a brilliant scoring record he was wasting away. No player wants to play reserve football and Niall's career was suffering. I am sure that he will be a great success at Maine Road and prove a lot of people wrong.

Transfer deadline day brought an amazing transfer deal to Highbury which eventually left Arsenal with egg on their faces, England's David Seaman confused and John Lukic an annoyed and bewildered goalkeeper. John has kept quiet about the saga but it seems that at eight o'clock in the morning of deadline day he received telephone call from the boss, telling him that

Seaman was being signed and that he was to go on loan to QPR until the end of the season. John said yes when half-asleep and then thought, "Why should I?"

There are many questions unanswered about that day. Why didn't the club speak to John first to discover if he wanted to go to Rangers? Why didn't they make it clear with QPR that Lukic had to go on loan to complete the deal and why was everything left until the last seconds? One thing that did emerge was John's character. He stood up to George and eventually, of course, moved on to Leeds.

I think that Arsenal have been fortunate to have had such a good character because Lukic could easily have thrown the towel in for the rest of the season. Had he been devious he might just have made Arsenal pay for treating him like a piece of machinery. There are a lot of players who would have lost interest but Lukic proved that he is 100 per cent a professional.

I accept that all we know is John's side of the story. There might have been a lot more going on behind the scenes and yet on the face of it, and to the public, it was a strange piece of man-management.

The title race has now reached the crisis stage. We have not played like Champions this season and yet we still have a chance of keeping the trophy although we must take maximum points from main rivals Aston Villa and Liverpool in two live TV games at Highbury.

Disaster, and we have blown it. We lost at home to Villa and only drew with Liverpool, John Barnes scoring a late goal to probably take the crown back to Anfield. They said they wanted it back and they meant business.

Between dropping four points to our rivals we only drew at FA Cup finalists Crystal Palace and then lost at Luton. We don't deserve anything on the back of that little run of results and it has meant a frustrating end to the season for everyone. All I have done is sit on the outside and watch the drama unfold again. Last season I saw us win it, this time I have been in the stand watching us fail to hold on.

The boss won't be happy. This was not in his plans at all. At the start of the season he drilled into us that he wanted to continue a winning era at Highbury and after three great seasons at Arsenal in which he has won the Littlewoods Cup, reached the same final and won the title, Arsenal have suddenly won nothing under George Graham. There is no panic, of course, but it is time for the boss perhaps to take stock again and set his stall out for a massive attack on three major competitions next season. We have proved that it is harder to hold on to the Championship than win it. You have to be able to cope with the pressure. The old saying is that it is tough at the top and Liverpool have proved that they are the only ones at the moment able to cope.

Liverpool have the secret – no one else does. God knows what it is but they can climb the mountain while others struggle. In the end we did not even come close. Arsenal, quite rightly, are expected to win something every season and the spotlight will be turned on even brighter when the kick-off comes around again in August. There is no question in my mind that the manager must bring in new faces. New expensive signings not only strengthen the team, they inspire others and lift a club with their presence and new qualities.

My own future as the season came to an end was obviously clouded. I have one more season under contract to Arsenal and would love to think that I could play in the first team throughout next season and be offered a new deal. But there have to be doubts and I am concerned that George Graham sees something in me that he doesn't particularly like.

It all adds up to a frustrating season for me. After the elation of winning the title, the ups and down of 1989-90 have pushed me back. I have had too many injuries, then came the death of my father and, of course, the bust-ups with the boss which I didn't enjoy and certainly didn't want to happen.

He has my future in his hands now because I am under contract. I want to play and stay but see no point if he is not going to make me a first-team regular. The last thing I want is to struggle around the reserves next season, at the age of 31. There would be no point in that and it would not do the club or me any good.

It didn't surprise me when Arsenal bought and sold in the summer of 1990. George Graham knew that he had to change things and out went Kevin Richardson, Martin Hayes and even assistant Theo Foley to take over at Northampton. In came

David Seaman, inevitably Andy Linighan, both for more than £1,000,000. And more new signings were certain. It only made me feel even more unsettled.

My recent experiences, however, have not put me off and I was happy to log what I have been through over the last few months and allow it to help me in the future, whatever that holds. As I have said, many of the people I have met have made an impact on me for different reasons. Chairmen, players, managers, friends have all helped in their own way to stand me in good stead. It has been an insight into football and George Graham has simply added to the experience.

My experiences have made me even more determined to do things my way. I was interested to read recently that John Wile, the former West Brom centre-half and skipper, said that he couldn't be a successful manager because he wasn't two-faced enough. If I ever become a manager I will be determined to carry honesty into my office. It is what players respect. Why treat people like doormats, why be devious to them? Deal with problems openly and don't make others suffer for the sake of your whim. I have discovered that the worst part of football is lack of communication.

One thing I am sure of is that whatever the future holds for Arsenal George Graham will do it his way. He has never worried about what people say, or been clouded by what others have done. He is the boss, like him or not, respect him or not. His record speaks for itself. George Graham goes down as one of the more interesting men I have met in my travels through football. It is a great experience and, as Howard Wilkinson proved to me at Hillsborough, it is the way it is.

Chapter Ten
WHY I MUST QUIT ARSENAL

ON 21 MAY 1990, at 7.55 a.m., my son, James William Marwood, was born. I was present at the birth and for the third time in my life I felt the pride, excitement and happiness of being a father. It is difficult to put into words how you feel when your child is born and for any man to have a son is a wonderful, special moment.

George Graham, as he has always been in moments like this, was brilliant. He didn't take me on Arsenal's end-of-season journey to Singapore, allowing me instead to stay behind to be with Lesley and help her with the girls. Not for the first time the boss showed that he has a warm heart when any of his players have personal problems. He was brilliant when I first joined Arsenal and we had problems with Sophie. Then he allowed me time off when my father died. I can't thank him enough and it is part of his man-management that I can't fault.

There is, however, another side of George Graham which is hard to work out. And it was that nagging feeling that I couldn't get out of my mind, even when James and Lesley came home from St Albans City General Hospital and the Marwood family enjoyed that lovely atmosphere a new-born baby brings.

I thought about George Graham and Arsenal a lot in the summer of 1990. I tossed over in my head what had happened to me during the season, how I had fallen from being a first-team player with a Championship medal to a man who didn't know if he wanted to play for one of the biggest clubs in the world any more, or its manager. I asked myself: Is it me, or him? Am I right or am I being over-sensitive?

It was the last thing I needed at a time like this. But I knew that I had to sort it out, one way or the other. I thought about all the good times I had had at Arsenal, the friends I had made and the fact that I had fought so long in my life to play for one of the 'giants' of football. However, I kept returning to the fact that George Graham had let me down one too many times. I couldn't forget the incidents, the little things he had said, the rumours and the uncomfortable feeling that dominated too many days last season.

I had never asked for a transfer in my life. I didn't really want to ask for one now but my thoughts kept returning to the inevitable conclusion. Deep down I wanted to spend the rest of my career at Arsenal but the things that happened to me last season, which I have explained in detail before, were too much of a worry. I believed that the manager was trying to phase me out of the team and, worse still, I didn't believe it when he denied that there was anything personal between us.

My last question to myself was: How long can you put up with this? By now you will appreciate that I am a man of principle and if I believe that something is right I do it. At my age I couldn't face the prospect of being a reserve player after being involved with the Championship side for so long. So one night I went to bed after more thoughts, more discussion, more heartache – with my mind made up. There was only one thing to do.

The following morning I made an appointment to see the manager and was told that it would be at Highbury on 19 June. There was no turning back now, I was going to ask Arsenal for a transfer.

How I would like the Arsenal fans to remember me.

George Graham and I met at one of the new executive boxes at Highbury because his office was out of bounds as a result of building work being carried out at the stadium. It was strange to look out on the pitch where I love playing and trying to explain my reasons for wanting to go. There is no point in hiding the truth and I have never been someone to mince his words. I explained that it had become more of a problem between us and I felt that it had become personal.

The boss, of course, denied that there was anything personal and didn't agree with me on anything I said. But there was no turning back and I had made up my mind to ask for a transfer. I couldn't tell if he was surprised or not because the boss is always "Mr Cool" in situations like this. He didn't put up a fight to make me change my mind. I said that I felt it was the time to leave the football club and he simply asked me to put my transfer request in writing.

That wasn't difficult because I already had written the letters and had two envelopes in my pocket, one for the boss and a second for chief executive, Ken Friar. George and I shook hands and I dropped one of my transfer requests into Mr Friar's office on the way out. I drove home feeling a sense of sadness that it had come to this, but relief that everything was now out in the open.

Not a word. Why haven't they replied? Am I going or not? I didn't hear anything from Arsenal for weeks and couldn't understand what the delay was about. Surely it is a simple thing to reply to. A player wants a transfer – can he go or is he staying?

Then on the morning of 16 July, the very day Arsenal reported back for pre-season training, a letter arrived at my home from the club. I read it as I prepared to start my third season as an Arsenal player and what I read disappointed me. Arsenal had turned down my request although the key phrase in the typed letter was that "at this present time" we can't grant your request. I hoped that the door was still open and drove to training slightly confused. If the manager doesn't pick me, why does he want me to stay?

George and I saw each other at training, of course, but he didn't pull me aside and explain anything. To this day there has been no explanation why Arsenal and George Graham wanted to keep me and our only communication has been little pleasant "good mornings" or training instructions.

I just hope he doesn't make me suffer. Reserve football is no good to me and the last thing I need at this stage of my career is a lot of playing in the reserves. I have one season left of my three-year contract and want to give everything to Arsenal, despite my request. I have doubts, however, whether George Graham will allow me to do that.

There were new faces in the Arsenal squad when the players reported back. John Lukic had gone to Leeds and was replaced by, surprise, surprise, David Seaman from Queen's Park Rangers. That was the worst-kept secret in football and George finally got his man. We have also signed Andy Linighan, the Norwich centre-half.

The most significant signing for me, alas, is the the arrival of Anders Limpar from Sweden, another £1-million-plus signing. It looks as though Limpar has been bought to play in my left-side position.

The pre-season tour to Sweden brought all my fears crashing down around me. I expected to be an odd man

Another award at Arsenal, this time the Player of the Month, but will there be any more?

out but it is always a shock when you realise that you are no longer first choice in the team. I played two half games in Sweden but it was the last and third game when I realised that I was to be one of many fringe players at Highbury. The boss had been working on the team he obviously saw as his number one and when he picked his side for that third game it was Limpar who was on the left side alongside Alan Smith and Paul Merson up front.

It looks as though George will start the season with a flat back four with Linighan alongside Tony Adams in the centre of defence and a midfield of David Rocastle, Michael Thomas and Paul Davis. This side looks strong and set and this will be the first time I have started a season not as a first choice. It is one of the reasons I asked for a transfer and I can't understand why the club have turned it down. There is so much talent, the depth of the pool is so strong, I don't believe they would miss me.

I shouldn't be disappointed about what is happening but I am. It is a bitter pill to swallow.

Professionally, I am ripped apart. All I want to do is play football and to be wanted. I have no regrets about asking for a transfer but what is loomimg ahead of me is not a mouth-watering prospect. Lesley and I have discussed things for hours and there is only one thing for me to do, keep my head up, retain my pride and maintain my fitness. The one thing that all this has done for me is to make me realise how important a stable and happy personal life is. It has been wonderful to be able to go home and close the door on all my concerns and worries.

Football does turn you on your head and things could happen. I have to stay with the belief that I might get back in the side, through injury or lack of form, or that suddenly a transfer might come my way. It will, however, be strange to train with the reserves under George Armstrong, the former Arsenal legend who has been brought back to take over from Theo Foley, George's assistant, who has gone to take over as manager of Northampton. Geordie has always been one of my favourite players and it is ironic that when I joined I was likened to him as a player. The manager even said that I could be Arsenal's new George Armstrong. But as Armstrong returns, I am on the way out.

My only hope is that the manager doesn't put me through misery. I heard how Charlie Nicholas, Kenny Sansom and Niall Quinn, who all wanted to quit, were made to languish in the reserves. I hope George Graham doesn't put me through that. With one year left of my contract, and by the time the agreement ends, I will be 31. There just doesn't seem any point in Arsenal waiting for that to run out. How much would they get for me if I was out of contract? Certainly not as much as if they sold me before my contract expired.

If this turns into a long drawn-out affair I will go mad with frustration.

The manager does know that if he picks me I will give Arsenal everything, I am a professional footballer and that must come before any other feeling. There is certainly more pressure on the manager than at any time in his career. Last season he didn't win anything for the first time and he has made three £1 million signings, the first time he has broken the magic six-figure sum. People will judge him on that and the expectancy is greater than ever before.

I hope he succeeds. I just wish I could be part of another Championship season because the memory of Anfield will live with me forever. But deep down, I believe that George and I know that there is no turning back for us. And he has made it clear that he doesn't see me as a long-term part of his plans. If he gets the right offer I just hope he will sell me.

All I ask is, don't make me suffer.

I have made it clear all through this book and my life story that I respect "big men" and a number of personalities have made an impression on me. George has certainly made a big impression on me, and I can't deny I have a great amount of respect for him, but sadly that has been tarnished slightly over the last twelve months.